Nine Days *in* Heaven

The vision of Marietta Davis

Nine Days *in* Heaven

The vision of Marietta Davis

DENNIS & NOLENE PRINCE

CREATION
HOUSE
A STRANG COMPANY

NINE DAYS IN HEAVEN By Dennis and Nolene Prince
Published by Creation House
A Strang Company
600 Rinehart Road
Lake Mary, Florida 32746

All Scripture quotations are from the Holy Bible, New International Version. Copyright © 1973, 1978, 1984, International Bible Society. Used by permission.

The vision of Marietta Davis was originally published as
Scenes Beyond the Grave by J. L. Scott (Dayton, OH: Stephen
Deuel, 1859), public domain.

Cover design by Terry Clifton

Library of Congress Control Number: 2005939106
International Standard Book Number: 978-1-59979-002-2

08 09 10 11 • SCC • 9 8 7 6 5 4 3 2
Printed in the United States of America

Contents

Preface vii

Introduction 1

1 The Angel of Peace 4

2 Death's Gateway 8

3 Welcome in Heaven 13

4 First Lessons and Warnings 18

5 The Boy Who Was Raised in Heaven 22

6 Heaven's Architecture 25

7 Conflicts in Hell 28

8 Despair of the Lost 32

9 The Intellectual, the False Teacher, and the Heartless
   Worshipers 40

10 Escape From Hell and Lessons Learned 50

11 The Music of Heaven and the Separation 53

12 Infant Instruction—the Lost Man 58

13 The Bethlehem Story 63

14 The Justice-Mercy Conflict 66

15 The Judas Betrayal 71

16 Jesus the Ransom Must Suffer 79

17 Apollyon 84

18 The Dream of Pilate's Wife 89

19 The Way of the Cross 92

20 The Thirty Pieces of Silver 97

21 Calvary 101

22 Death Defeated 104

23 He Is Risen! 110

24 The Lost Man Rescued 115

25 Return to Earth 119

    Appendix A: Original Testimonials 122

    Appendix B: Infant Paradise 130

    Notes 145

Our first child died suddenly when he was four months old. We hoped the pain of that event would be swept away with the birth of our second baby seventeen months later, but this little one, a girl, was stillborn at full term.

So we felt the full force of the lot that befalls those who lose a child. The shock, the tears, the pain, the numbness, the questions, the turmoil, the fear. Each seemed to take its turn in never-ending waves.

Family and friends were wonderful as they gathered around us. One of these friends was a lady a few years older than us. Her name was Elva. Elva sidled up to Nolene and myself one day and gave us a brown paper parcel. In it was an old copy of the book *Scenes Beyond the Grave* by John Loughran Scott, which recounts the vision of Marietta Davis. She thought it would help.

It did. It was as though we were transported from our tired earth to a place way up there—a place of liberation and under-standing—where we could see just as God sees. A place from where we could approach our lives with a new conviction that God was in control, that all was well with our two children and that we could trust God with our tomorrows.

I wondered why the whole world didn't know about this book. But even as I wondered, I knew the reason. The difficult language, unusual even for that time, made it almost unreadable. You could follow the story if you worked at it, but many parts were incomprehensible without a dictionary in your hand. I wondered why someone had not rewritten it in a way it could be understood.

For years I took it with me to read on holidays. Each time I did, I thought that one day, when work was quiet, I might rewrite it myself. It never did get quiet so I began anyway, hoping to complete it in one year. It took three, working first with a dictionary and thesaurus, and then with a red pen on progressive rewrites. My wife, Nolene, seeing my frustrations, joined me. A lover of crosswords and word games and a voracious reader, she was invaluable.

In my opinion, the whole world should read this story. Some find it strange and hard to believe. Thousands have been inspired and challenged. But everyone should read it— and with an open mind. As the original publisher raved in the conservative language of 150 years ago, "to read it is to be benefited."

—DENNIS PRINCE

Introduction

MARIETTA DAVIS WAS born in 1823, in Berlin, New York, where she lived with her mother and two sisters. At twenty-five years of age she experienced a vision that made her the talking point of her community and a legend for generations to come.

Her story was put into print and the original publisher observed cautiously, "Edition after edition has been published and passed silently into the hands of the reading public." And so the remarkable story became widely known.

A hundred years later the book was still in print, but the difficult language led to a decline in its popularity. It was wordy, complex, and flowery—far more so than the language of the time. Modern readers baulked at words like *fain, preponderating, effulgence, habiliments, dissever, behooves,* and *vouchsafed;* and phrases such as "a sable veil of nether night," "indulgence of propensities and reversion of the movement of destructive tendency." Only the most tenacious readers made it to the end and most of them missed many gems that were hidden in the difficult words and phrases.

This book is an attempt to capture the original story in the language of today. In making this rewrite, every effort has been made to preserve the original intent of the story. The reader will find some sections a little formal, a hangover from the original language that was difficult to erase completely without compromising the integrity of the original. In spite of this, the story retains its interest and fascination.

The following background has been summarized from the supporting testimonials of the original publisher, family, attending physician, Marietta's pastor, and other ministers of the day. These testimonials appear in close to their original form at the end of this book.

Background to the Story

A religious revival in their hometown had impacted the lives of Marietta's mother and sisters but had left Marietta unaffected. Although she had thought about the issues involved, she was not a religious person and was not interested in discussing these things.

Seven months after the revival Marietta suddenly and unexpectedly fell into a trance, which, remarkably, lasted nine days. During this time her family and their doctors were unable to rouse her. When she finally regained consciousness she had full control of her faculties and described with almost supernatural perception how angels had conducted her spirit to heaven and hell. She described extraordinary scenes from these places in graphic detail.

Marietta made it plain that her vision was given for a specific reason. She had been instructed to tell the world so that men and women could prepare for the next life.

Marietta died seven months after the vision—at the time and in the manner she predicted.

Visions and Trances in the Bible

I was praying and "in a trance I saw a vision."
— THE APOSTLE PETER, ACTS 11:5

When I was praying "I fell into a trance and saw the Lord speaking."
— THE APOSTLE PAUL, ACTS 22:17–18

After this I looked, and there before me was a door standing open in heaven. And the voice I had first heard speaking to me like a trumpet said, "Come up here, and I will show you what must take place after this."
— THE APOSTLE JOHN, REVELATION 4:1

I know a man in Christ who fourteen years ago was caught up to the third heaven. Whether it was in the body or out of the body I do not know—God knows. And I know that this man—whether in the body or apart from the body I do not know, but God knows—was caught up to paradise. He heard inexpressible things, things that man is not permitted to tell.
— THE APOSTLE PAUL, SPEAKING OF HIMSELF
2 CORINTHIANS 12:2–4

In the last days, God says, I will pour out my Spirit on all people. Your sons and daughters will prophesy, your young men will see visions, your old men will dream dreams.
— ACTS 2:17

One

The Angel of Peace

"**W**HAT IS HAPPENING to me?"

The thought exploded in my mind as I reeled at the sight of the vast, bottomless deep beneath me.

"Am I dreaming? Am I dead? Am I alive?" A thousand questions raced through my mind as strange unidentifiable objects floated around me. I blinked, trying to clear my vision, but it was like a wild dream, with no familiar point of reference to which I could anchor my sanity.

"Help me! Help me!" My cry erupted from my deepest being as I gazed in despair at the endless, trackless space around me, and struggled in vain to return to the security of my country, my home, and my family.

A brilliant light appeared far above me. Like a giant star, its shaft of light thrust back the gloom as it steadily descended. My whole being was bathed in a glorious glow.

Gingerly I moved closer as it resolved itself into the most magnificent being I had ever seen. On her head was a crown of clustered jewels of light. In her left hand she held a simple cross. A saber of light was grasped in her right hand, and as she advanced toward me light streamed from it and touched me.

Instantly a whole new world of sensations filled my being. Fears and uncertainties were swept away and I was filled with an overpowering desire to go with her. Yet, paralyzed with awe and wonder, I could only stand and stare. Oddly, all my mind could think of was, *What is her name?* But as I stood there gaping, she spoke.

"So, Marietta! You would like to know who I am?" She smiled. "I am the Angel of Peace. I have been sent to show you what happens to humans when they leave this world. If you would like to know the answer to this question, follow me."

My mind was racing. How did I get myself into this? What had I done to bring me to this alien place?

*   *   *   *   *

For a long time before this I had wrestled with the great questions of life. A few things had become clearer as I had tossed them over and over in my mind, and I had reached a number of simple conclusions. These were: chasing money and fine things can never make you happy; relationships can let you down (no one is perfect); and many religious traditions are unreliable.

As I had looked around me I could plainly see that many people were unhappy and were craving peace. I had thought long and questioned hard, trying to learn about the human soul and why it behaves as it does. The more I had thought about these things the more I realized that I could not find the answers by myself. I passionately wanted answers, especially to the biggest question of all: "What happens to us when we die?" But I was unable to reach any satisfying conclusions. So it was, in the midst of this turmoil, that I found myself here on this strangest of strange days.

It had all begun slowly and gradually. I had progressively become less and less conscious of the physical things around me. My inner self seemed to become stronger and somehow more aware. The objects in the room—the walls, ceiling, and furniture—turned to shadows and finally disappeared altogether. I then found myself in this amazing new world with the extraordinary experiences it brought me.

Since returning, I have had many people ask me what happened. I have tried hard to tell them, because that is why I was shown all these things, but I struggle over the task. There is simply no way on earth to fully describe the things beyond earth. Our words even spoil the beauty and perfection of the heavenly things that are out there.

But I must complete the task I have been given, so I will try to describe what I saw. All I ask is that you who are reading this will look beyond my woefully inadequate words and try to see something of the true power, the graphic beauty, and divine glory of the things I saw.

* * * * *

"Follow me," said the angel, "but before you do, look back and see yourself."

I looked far below through the dark misty space and finally made out my motionless body. Gathered around me were my worried friends calling to me and frantically shaking me, trying every possible way to wake me, but without success.

"This is the human view of life," said my angelic guide. "Look at your family. They love you and grieve for you. Every human goes through troubles and heartbreaks, and ultimately death. But the true picture of what happens after that is hidden from them.

"Look out there at the world's teeming millions. They are full of hope, ambition, and troubles. Then finally, death arrives. All of them are afraid of death. It is a ruthless destroyer and cuts life short. Generations come and go, one after another in rapid succession."

Timidly I asked a question. "I know I am young and don't know much, but I have been thinking a lot about these things. One day all these people will die. What happens to them? Do they have a place to go to? Can you take me to them? Can I go and be with my loved ones who have already died?"

I waited for her answer. I realized how incredibly much I wanted to know it. For so long this question had haunted me, day and night. Unable to share it, I had buried it deep inside me where it went round and round, the answer always elusive. Now, unexpectedly and remarkably, this Angel of Peace stood before me, sent from the next world. I was on the brink of a monumental discovery, one that would at last settle these issues that had plagued me.

Two

Death's Gateway

THE ANGEL SPOKE. "Marietta, you have been given a special favor to learn about these things. First of all, let me tell you this. When people die they are taken to the place where they will spend the rest of eternity. However, the destiny of some is enormously different from the destiny of others."

As if to explain, she lifted her head and said, "Look up there. What can you see?"

I looked above me and saw a vast shining heavenly place, brighter by far than the sun at its peak. Dazzling light radiated from it, shooting across the heavenly skies. I was spellbound, and stared at it in wonder.

"There are many people up there you would love to see," said my guide. "They wear soft white clothes and live in unalloyed happiness. There is no night, no sorrow or death, no sin or pain, no suffering of any kind." She was silent for a moment. "However, before you see this, I have to show you some things that are not as pleasant.

"Marietta, you are well aware that people on earth have widely different values and morals. You may not be aware that when they die and their spirit lives on, their moral nature is not changed. The bad are still bad, but the good continue to be good."

She touched my forehead saying, "Tell me what you can see now."

A new scene opened up before me—vivid and graphic. I saw endless crowds of all kinds of people struggling in the throes of death. Some were in majestic palaces, lying on beds spread with fine and costly coverings. Some were in poor, humble cottages, while others lay in dark prisons. Some were in lonely forests, others in barren deserts or on raging seas. Some lay under the scorching sun, others were perishing on bleak snow-covered mountains. Some were surrounded by weeping friends, others were dying alone and forgotten. Some had been murdered; others were killed on the battlefield.

This was the place where time met eternity, and it was a place of indescribable misery.

"This is death," said my guide. "It is the result of a divine law that has been broken. But what you see here is only a small fraction of it."

She touched me with her saber of light, and as she did I found I could see the immortal nature of all the dying people. I was able to see their spirits. I stood fascinated as I watched them leave their bodies and enter the regions of eternity, tentatively stepping out into new and untried experiences.

Then I noticed that spirits of different kinds were gathered around each dying form. They were there to meet the earthly spirits as they entered the new regions. People of all classes and types were met—some by evil and wretched spirits, others by bright and holy angels sent from God. This gateway of death was the common transition state between earth and eternity.

As the people left their bodies they were attracted to spirits of a similar moral nature. Evil and unholy people joined like-minded spirits and then moved off towards regions that were covered by dark clouds. People who loved good and had formed relationships with good people were escorted by holy angels to the heavenly glories above.

I watched spellbound as all these spirits mingled together undergoing these strange experiences for the first time. I wondered if it was all just a dream.

Reading my thoughts, my guide took my hand. "These people have just left their bodies and will now begin a new existence. The change from physical to spiritual existence is very new and strange for them. But you, Marietta, will learn more about all this later. We have to leave this now and go to that shining heavenly place you saw before." With that she took my arm and we sped toward the cloud of light.

Having passed through this intermediate zone she stopped again and touched my eyes. I looked in wonder as new and different scenes opened up before me.

"Look!" she said. "Look at all those planets, the rolling heavens, the suns and systems of suns. See how they move in complete silence and perfect harmony. It is a huge expanse of universes built in infinite wisdom. Happy, holy people live in these—at different stages of development and different degrees of spirituality. These people will never die again."

Once again she touched my eyes, and immediately above me, around me, and far away I saw spirits of pure light passing us, travelling at the speed of thought.

"These are serving angels," my guide told me as they passed. "More than anything else they love to go on trips of mercy. They are protectors and messengers to people below them."

As I was watching them come and go, an angel passed close by, holding in her arms a baby spirit. The baby lay nestled in calm security, obviously well aware of its safety in the arms of its protector. We attracted the angel's attention and asked where the baby had come from.

"I received it from its mother," the angel replied. "She was brokenhearted. I am taking it to the infants' heaven in the Paradise of Peace."

As the angel passed us we moved silently in the same direction. I lost sight of the scenes below and my attention was drawn by the bright light of the heaven that we were approaching.

We stopped on a plain filled with trees laden with fruit.

We passed beneath their shady branches and I heard birds singing. Their beautiful melodies filled me with delight. They were the sweetest songs I had ever heard. I thought we must have been on some planet, so I asked the angel its name.

"This is the outer region of the spiritual paradise," she told me. "These trees, flowers, and birds are so pure and refined that humans cannot see them. Their eyes are veiled from it all. Their hearing is dulled too, so they cannot hear the sounds. In fact they don't even believe such pure and perfect things exist. You can see and hear them because you have left your body and can now experience them through your spiritual senses.

"Remember," she said, "that this region is only the outer boundary of the home of spirits. These are the lower levels of the homes of those who have been made holy. When redeemed people die, this is the first place they are brought to. Here their guardian protectors teach them the basics of eternal life. They learn about heaven and pure love, which is love not contaminated by sin. They meet old friends here— those who have preceded them and have advanced spiritually to take on higher tasks. Family members can meet them here and talk with them for the first time.

"This is the place where they first learn to sing the song of redeeming grace. They can rest here too and enjoy the pure atmosphere."

It was all so strange, but I was utterly absorbed. I found myself yearning to meet friends I had lost long ago, but the angel said, "You are not allowed to stay here. You have to learn what happens to people after they die. When your earth-life finally ends you will come back and be with your family. Then you will begin your immortal state and be taught how to prepare for higher things."

With that she picked a rose, held it for me to smell the fragrance and touched my lips with it. My eyes were opened further and I saw many, many happy people moving everywhere through the flowery landscapes. I desperately wanted to join

11

them but my guide moved forward and upward, through forests which became purer and more beautiful with each moment.

As we rose, a thousand questions flooded my mind. I was overwhelmed by the beauty of the place we were leaving yet the angel had referred to it as only the outer boundary, the region of lower homes. How could anything be more beautiful? Then my mind went back to what I had seen earlier. What of the dark clouds where the other spirits had been taken? What lay behind them? It was overwhelming, unexpected, and yet real. I was filled with a mixture of apprehension, fascination, and anticipation.

Three

Welcome in Heaven

W E MOVED ON until, in the distance, I saw a domed pavilion of light. "That is the gate to the City of Peace," my guide told me.

"We are going there now and..." She paused. "You will meet your Redeemer."

She continued. "It is a beautiful place. Angels live there, and also the people whom God has made holy. They love to play golden harps, lyres, and other stringed instruments. They sing the song of redemption over and over. It is the song of peace and never ending love."

As we drew closer, a group of angels even more glorious than the ones I had seen gathered around the gateway to the city. We approached them and their leader spoke to my guide in a language I could not understand.

The gate was made of jasper and diamonds. It opened and two angelic beings approached me. I was trembling with fear, but they each took me by the hand and led me toward another gate, which led directly to the pavilion of light. I could not speak. The sight of this perfect beauty and holiness was beyond description.

As I tried to take it all in I was suddenly overcome by my sinful state and rebellious nature. My mind flooded with memories of past sins and doubts. Unable to cope with the sheer glory of everything around me I fell to the ground. Then the angelic attendants gently picked me up and carried me through the elaborate doorway. They placed me at the feet of the most glorious Being I could ever imagine. A crown of pure light rested on His head, and hair, white as snow, fell upon His shoulders. No words could begin to describe His splendor.

An attending angel spoke quietly to me. "Marietta, this is your Redeemer. He is God. Yet He put aside His divinity and came to earth as a man, and suffered for your sins. He died for you outside the gate of Jerusalem. (See Hebrews 13:11–12.) He died alone, just as it was written centuries before: '[he trod] the winepress alone.' (Isa. 63:3)."[1]

I was totally overawed by Him. His goodness, tenderness, and love overwhelmed me. I bowed down, feeling that if I could only be considered worthy I would worship Him.

He reached out His hand and lifted me up. "Welcome, my child." The sound of His voice penetrated deep inside me and filled me with a joy that I cannot begin to describe. "Come for a while into the home of the redeemed," He said. Then, turning to those around, He added, "Make her welcome."

Immediately the whole gathering stood to their feet and, with loving humility, embraced me as one of themselves, an heir of God's grace. Then, taking up their musical instruments, they sang a superb anthem. The music sounded like the rush of many waters and it filled the entire dome. At the conclusion, the echo faded slowly into the distance, like gentle waves which seemed to carry me along with them.

The moment was broken when a spirit moved out from the gathering and called my name, "Marietta!" I was overwhelmed to find myself in the embrace of someone I had loved very dearly on earth. "Welcome," she cried. "Welcome to our home of peace." "Welcome, three times welcome!" echoed the music of a thousand voices. Others had gathered all around me, people I had known and loved on earth, all eager to greet me and hug me.

We found ourselves in a large beautiful room where we

relaxed together as only old and familiar friends can do. I recognized all of them instantly, but they were very different from the way I remembered them on earth. I cannot describe them properly except to say that they seemed to be all mind, all light, all glory, all adoration, all love supremely pure, all peace, and calm serenity. All of these qualities were woven together in an awe-inspiring heavenly way.

They talked freely with each other, but not in human language. They spoke without sound, thought to thought and spirit to spirit. Ideas flowed from being to being and I learned there and then that in heaven you cannot hide things! Harmony was in everything—in sound, desire, speech, in songs of adoration. Harmony was their life, their love, their appearance, and their supreme delight.

Then they sang another song, a lively hymn of redemption to their Maker's name. My guide tried to persuade me to join in, but I could not. I was too absorbed in thinking about this long-sought home of rest, and experiencing its glory. When they finished singing they kissed me, one after another, eager to hold me. They embraced me as a newborn soul, thanking their Redeemer and Lord as they did. It was wonderful!

"So this is heaven!" I cried. "And all these happy people— are they really the ones I knew? They used to struggle so hard in their old human bodies. Look at their faces now! The glory of this place has made them absolutely radiant! They used to look so worried! And whatever happened to the ravages of old age?"

I remember now how often I used to listen to my pastor on earth as he attempted to describe the glories of eternal life. Sometimes he would grieve when he realized that most of the people listening still didn't understand. I used to ask, "Can heaven really be so glorious? Haven't you exaggerated it? And if men and women truly can get to heaven," I scoffed, "will they really bathe in sunshine?" Rest assured, even the wildest imaginations of people do not begin to approach the reality and pleasures of that glorious place.

As I pondered, a man approached me. I remembered him from earth. Old and gaunt, he had faithfully followed the Redeemer during his life, but through many trials. His grey hair had told the story of a life of sorrow and trouble. How different he was now! His spirit stood upright and confident before me, a picture of immortal youth. Gone was the walking stick, the gaunt trembling frame, the grief-worn cheek, the hollow eye, the sick body. In their place were light, health, and vigor.

"Look at me now!" he cried. "Look what redeeming grace has done! This heart of mine was once a cage of unholy thoughts. These hands were once occupied in wrongdoing. These feet once walked on a fast downhill road that ended in sorrow and death. This body of mine—no not this body, but the old one I left behind—was worn with grief, corrupted by sin, and dying from disease.

"But now! All hail that name, Immanuel! I am redeemed through Him and I wear these marvelous clothes of light and live in never-ending youth. This is my song now:

> "O death, where is your sting, and grave,
> Where is your victory? (1 Cor. 15:55)
> Worthy is the Lamb who offered Himself to redeem us!
>   He is worthy!
> O give Him adoration you countless hosts,
> You innumerable throng!
> Worship and adore Him all people! Let the whole
>   universe adore Him!
> Adore Him, because He is worthy to receive songs of
>   universal praise!"

A group of children ran forward. They joined hands and danced around singing:

> "Praise Him! Yes! Look!

When He was on earth He said,
'Let the little children come to me,
And do not forbid them. Yes!
Do not stop them,
Let them come to me' (Matt. 19:14)."

Four

First Lessons and Warnings

THE SONG FINISHED and I looked up to see the dome above me opening and more beings approaching. They were even more glorious than those I had seen before, and the light of their glory overwhelmed me. I turned away from them and rushed to my guide who said to me, "Marietta, this is only a foretaste of the happy things to come. You have been welcomed here and have seen your Redeemer. But look above you," she urged, "the glory of the cross is coming down. The people with it are redeemed spirits of your race who have gone on to a higher life."

So I looked up and saw above me a cross, carried by a group of twelve people. Around them were written the words: "Patriarchs, Prophets, and Apostles" and above them, "Jesus of Nazareth, King of the Jews." Bowing at the foot of the cross was a spirit dressed in white clothes. Her face glowed with an expression of undivided holy adoration.

She kissed the cross and then descended to me. "Welcome, to you who come from the sad world below. Please listen, because Jesus my Lord and Redeemer wants me to talk to you. He has permitted you to come here for this short time. You will have to return to your friends on earth again when your mission is complete. But don't be sad," she said, looking at me with understanding.

The sudden thought of going back to the sins and troubles

of my old life so affected me that I felt as though I was leaving that divine place right then and plummeting back to earth. But, seeing my distress, my angel guide embraced me and said, "You have to do this, Marietta. When you return you will take with you the message of God's holy love. Later, at a chosen time and when you are free from mortality, you will come back permanently to this holy company."

The spirit continued, "Marietta, you have been brought here for a special purpose. I am here to teach you many things about heaven and earth. I know the thought of returning makes you sad, but you will go back loaded with experiences and truths to teach others.

"The first thing you must learn is that all of heaven reveres the cross. Tens of thousands bow before it. The redeemed ones love to linger around it. Worship on earth is very dreary compared with the worship here," she added.

"This spiritual heaven begins just above the plains of earth and guardian spirits are constantly moving around it. On earth these countless unseen guardian angels mingle with people as they are permitted. There is not a day, an hour, nor a moment when any mortal is not watched by the spirit appointed to him." She paused and went on.

"Man does not understand sin. Nor does he understand how great God's grace is in providing redemption. There are many, many things preventing the light of heaven from reaching mankind, but the time is getting close when people will become more aware of the reality of this place. Then they will look more carefully at spiritual truth. Man's final redemption is getting close."

She continued, "Watch very closely, for you are about to have implanted in your mind a tiny part of the joy that fills this land." She explained further, "Did you notice when I came down that I kissed the cross? We love to do that. It is an expression of our love for the Redeemer."

She paused, and out of the silence I heard soft and beautiful *alleluias* in the distance. "Who is that singing?" I asked.

"They are the ones who have come out of the great tribulation," she replied. "They never stop singing anthems to exalt their Savior's name—night and day.[1] Would you like to live here forever? Would you like to join these singers?" she asked.

"Before you do, I must warn you about the unbelief and lack of faith and dedication you showed on earth. For there is no other way apart from Christ, the Redeemer, to find an inheritance in this place."

As she reminded me of my former doubts and my lack of confidence in the Savior, I lost heart. I knew it was true and I cried out, "Is there any hope for me? Or has my chance to receive heaven gone? I would be so happy if I never went back to earth again. If only I could live here forever!"

"Be faithful then," said the spirit, "to the light given to you and you will eventually enjoy heaven." She then drew my attention to something else.

"Marietta, this will interest you. Here we can see the prophets and martyred saints. In the left hand of each there is a golden censer and in the right hand a small book."

Crowds were gathered around a tall pyramid made of pearls and extremely precious stones, set with crosses of diamonds. On these were engraved the names of those who spoke the truth of the gospel and for this suffered persecution and even death. Three spirits stood on the pyramid. Above them they held a cross from which floated a banner that seemed to unfurl endlessly.

"These spirits are specially chosen," my guide told me. "One is a patriarch, one a prophet, and one an apostle. They are commissioned saints who will be with the Son of Man when He returns to earth. On that day, these three will gather together the selected people from the four winds, from the most distant part of earth to the most distant part of heaven."

I looked at the books held by the spirits and my guide told me that they described the order of creation, the redemption of man, and the principles which govern the obedient.

Five

The Boy Who Was Raised in Heaven

A S THIS SCENE passed from my view, the spirit who had kissed the cross motioned with her hand, and two children came forward. They each took her hand and smiled shyly at her.

Turning to me she said, "These children died as babies. Being innocent ones, they were brought to paradise."

The older one looked at me. "Marietta, we are really happy to be able talk to you because you will eventually go back to those who loved us and mourned when we died. When you see them again, would you please give a message to the man who is now sitting beside your body on earth? Tell him that, although our parents may grieve for us, we are free and extremely happy. Tell them that this is the only world we know. It was here that we first awoke to the reality of our existence. Our guardian angels take us to visit earth, but it is not at all like heaven. We see sorrow, pain, and death there. Here in heaven there is harmony, happiness, and life."

The boy became silent, and looked down as if he was thinking deeply. I thought he seemed sad, but then I realized he was watching an angel coming up past us, close by. As I looked I was overwhelmed by what I saw. Light covered her like beautifully made clothing and she moved with perfect grace. I longed to follow her. "Who is she?" I said. "She is so glorious—I can feel it. I would so much like to meet her."

The spirit answered, "This is an angel who belongs to the Infant Paradise. Do you remember reading in the Gospel what the Redeemer said concerning little children? It says, "Their angels in heaven always see the face of my Father in heaven" (Matt. 18:10).

"This angel is a guardian protector of infants, and is commissioned to meet baby spirits as they leave earth and enter into the spiritual world. Look, she is slowing down for you and holding out her arms. What can you see, Marietta?"

"A small pale light," I answered.

The angel then breathed on it as if imparting life. She embraced it with a fondness far beyond that shown by earthly mothers and I could sense that the little spirit was at rest. I felt the glory that surrounded and pervaded the angel and I yearned to fly away with that baby and live happily forever. But the angel rose up beyond me and with a flash of light disappeared.

Then I saw a completely different scene. Below me in a little room I saw a woman kneeling by the lifeless body of her dead child. Her body shook as she wept. Tears were streaming from her eyes. Then she stopped crying and her face became like marble, her eyes set and glassy. Her whole body quivered as she pressed kiss after kiss on the cold cheek of her lost baby.

A man dressed in black entered solemnly, and silently approached the weeping mother. Taking her hand he said, "Come dear one. Try to understand that 'the LORD gave and the LORD has taken away; may the name of the LORD be praised' (Job 1:21). Remember that Jesus said, 'Let the little children come to me, and do not hinder them, for the kingdom of heaven belongs to such as these' (Matt. 19:14). Jesus also told us that 'their angels in heaven always see the face of my Father in heaven' (Matt. 18:10)."

The scene changed and I saw the mother sitting beside a coffin with a gathering of people. She was staring at the ceiling, her face filled with grief. In front of the coffin stood the solemn man whom I had seen before. He read a Psalm, prayed for the distressed, and then endeavored to encourage the mourners by explaining from the Bible that the baby, though dead, would live again, and that an angel had taken it to Abraham's tender care. (See Luke 16:22.)

The scene eventually faded and the boy said to me, "That lifeless form you just saw in the vision was my body, and the weeping woman was my mother. This is what happened after I left my body. The solemn man was a Christian minister. The passing angel who paused before us just now was the one who carried me to the place prepared for young and fragile children. These angel spirits are continually nourishing their little minds."

At this point in the original book there follow four chapters which describe in lengthy detail how angels nurture and teach small infants in a special nursery in paradise. In order to maintain a consistent pace throughout the story, these four chapters, which are self-contained, have been placed at the end of the book. (See Appendix B.)

Six

Heaven's Architecture

A VOICE ABOVE US called, "Come up here!"

A chariot-like cloud of light picked us up, and we rose inside a circular area rather like the interior of a tower. Its spiral walls formed galleries, winding ever upward and it seemed to be formed of rainbows wreathed in spirals of prismatic shades. Each one reflected many beautiful colors of matchless luster.

A profound sense of peace and delight filled me as we emerged at the top. We found ourselves on an aerial plain suspended above the lofty dome of the central temple. From here I could see the complete layout of the great city, stretching out on every side. Its beauty was breathtaking.

Beneath me was the infants' Temple of Instruction. Built of the most precious materials it was an architectural wonder, rising from the center of a vast circular lawn of soft, lush, green grass. Spaced at regular intervals were groups of majestic trees with luxuriant clusters of fragrant flowers. Beneath them in the open spaces were tiny garden beds filled with every variety of flower, blossoming shrubs, and vines.

Fountains of dancing waters caught my eye. Some bubbled up from the green grass to flow with a low and pleasant murmur through marble channels or beds of golden sand. Others gushed up very high, cascading down in streams which fed into basins. Some of these basins looked like diamonds, others like polished silver or the whitest pearl.

The circular lawn was surrounded by high, open trelliswork with a gateway at its eastern side. Flowing out through the gateway was a river, supplied by the fountains within.

Looking around at the surrounding city, I noticed it was divided into twelve great divisions by this river. The river flowed in a spiral course, in twelve huge curves proceeding out from the center to the circumference. On each side of the river was a wide avenue and twelve other straight streets intersected this spiral avenue. The straight streets began in the consecrated ground about the temple and radiated out to twelve equally divided points on the outer boundary. So the city was divided into one hundred and forty-four great suburbs, or divisions, arranged in increasing degrees of magnificence and beauty.

As my gaze followed the pathway of the flowing river and the stately avenues I lost all sense of time and self awareness. I had never seen anything like it in its splendor and complexity and I became completely absorbed in studying it.

Each building in the city was extremely large and perfectly integrated with all the others. The entire city gave the impression of being one garden of flowers, one grove of shady trees, one gallery of sculptures, and one sea of fountains. All of these, together with the buildings, formed an unbroken expanse of sumptuous architecture set in a surrounding landscape of matching beauty. This was then overarched by a colored sky that bathed every object in its incredible and ever-changing shades.

After a time I became aware of the inhabitants. But I can give only the faintest picture of what was before me. I would describe it by saying that the way the angelic multitude moved together was like a single melody, animated by one inspiring love, and moving in one orderly plan. Their unchanging focus was the development of their infant charges to the same state of perfection as that of the city.

The melody of their movement was echoed in the groups of

infants, where there was no rivalry or desire for selfish glory. Rather, each group in each nursery was united to the more mature groups. In some way I could sense that each little child was filled with holy love and a desire to grow in wisdom, to be capable of being used as an angel of light and loveliness. I could see that each one loved to learn from those above them and they were devoting themselves completely to unselfish acts of love.

In this way I saw each little child unfold like petals of a flower from beauty to beauty. All above them was glory. All around them was loveliness. All within them was the melody of unfolding life, unfolding love, unfolding knowledge of heaven, adoration of the Savior, and the inspiration of eternal joy.

At this point my guide spoke to me and turned me away from this scene. "Marietta, you have now seen the wonders of the first and most simple stage of paradise, where the infants are taught." She looked at me solemnly. "But before you can go any further there is a sobering lesson you have to receive."

Seven

Conflicts in Hell

S HE TOUCHED MY forehead and immediately the brightness and glory vanished and I began to descend. I found myself passing through a low and gloomy subterranean vault, surrounded by thick folds of darkness. A feeling of supernatural dread came over me and I began to shake spasmodically. A terrible conflict rose up within me and filled my being. I was startled and confused and my thoughts shattered into utter chaos.

As I fell further, I heard a distant roar. It sounded as if an ocean was pouring down some rocky cataract. I flailed about, trying in vain to grab something to slow my fall which was taking me toward the awful abyss below.

At this moment a blue sulphurous flash lit up the darkness. As it disappeared I stared in disbelief as grim specters floated around me, enveloped by fires of evil. Gone was the holiness and peace that had surrounded the dwellers in paradise. The change was so sudden and dreadful I could not think clearly. My mind was flooded with horror and despair. I was terrorstruck! I turned to my guide for help, but she was gone!

Alone and in that dreadful place there are no means by which I can give even a faint idea of the agony of that moment. At first I thought I would pray, but as I began, my whole life flashed before me in an instant and I realized I was utterly unworthy of God's favor. I cried out, "Oh! If I could have only one hour back on earth—for a time, just a brief time—to make myself fit for heaven!"

Like a monster my conscience struck back at me. "You had your chance! In your time on earth you turned your back on the provision God made for your sins. You completely rejected it! Do you think now in this place of darkness and woe that your plea could possibly succeed?"

To add to my misery, all my previous doubts and skepticism then rose up like animals, glaring at me and encircling me in condemning mockery. All of my life's thoughts reared up with them. Not one of my secrets was hidden—they were all there. Even the ones I had forgotten stood plainly before me.

At first they came one at a time, but then they all combined and took on my own character. I was facing myself! To escape them was to run from myself. To annihilate them would have blotted out my own existence.

I was stunned as the words of the Savior echoed through my mind, "Men will have to give account on the day of judgment for every careless word they have spoken" (Matt. 12:36).

I reeled back in turmoil, longing to escape and return to my body, but another scene appeared before me—the most terrible scene of all. It was a clear and dramatic vision of my crucified Redeemer. As it appeared, all the misconceptions I'd ever had about Jesus passed before my mind in the form of pictures.

In one picture I saw those thoughts in which I had viewed Jesus as only a man. In another were my beliefs about the "doctrine" of special forgiveness for a limited number of people who were "chosen." Along with this I saw the tears I had once shed when I believed I was doomed to an endless punishment because I thought this had been predestined for me.

Then in another picture was the idea I had once entertained that eternal salvation would be given out freely to everybody—without any need for moral change and without a personal and loving faith in the Savior's death for our sins. And in still in another, I saw my ideas about obtaining salvation simply through living a good life.

These separate pictures blended into one spinning mass around me. In it were ten thousand confused images of everything I had ever learned or imagined about Christ, heaven, hell, religion, or eternal life. All my ideas of the Redeemer were related to one another, yet they conflicted in so many ways. I was completely bewildered by it all.

I saw in each image a distorted view of the Savior. But none of them, either singly or together, showed Him as He really is. None of them showed His divine glory, His honor, His majesty, His perfection. None of them demonstrated His exalting and redeeming power. I, Marietta Davis, was simply not able to see Him in His true character, as Prince and Savior.

Totally overwhelmed, I was ready to give up all hope of ever escaping that place. I concluded this warped view of the Savior would be my last—a sight that would fill my cup of woe to the brim. I had already drunk from it and it would last me for all eternity.

But then I saw Him—suddenly, unexpectedly—in the midst of a cloud, stretching His arms toward me. He spoke with a voice of love, inviting me, even as burdened and as faulty as I was, "Come to me" (Matt. 11:28).

What a contrast it was! That glorious Being, surrounded by radiance as bright as the sun and circled by a revolving halo of light. I could clearly see His relationship to the universe of light where the angels live. I could also see the awful disparity between my own corrupt nature and that wonderful place of light and life, harmony and love. So I saw Him, the Holy One. Him in the brightness of His glory, the one I had rejected so many times in my madness, in my foolishness, in my skepticism.

I gazed at Him and realized how desperately I wanted to break away from the tormenting mental forces that surrounded me. I wanted to go to paradise and live there in its beauty, peace, and joy. But there was such a gulf between that holy place and my impure, fallen mind that I could not do it, and all my doubts overwhelmed me once again.

Despair of the Lost

ITH THIS, A gloomy black veil of night rose up from below. My doubts formed a cloud that shut out the glory from above and plunged me into a vortex of gloom. I fell rapidly, and the surrounding darkness opened to receive me.

Eventually, in the furthest depths I saw a vast unending plain which appeared to be covered with sparkling vegetation. Glowing objects, like waving trees with thick foliage and flowers and fruits of crystal and gold, could be seen in every direction.

Crowds of spirits appeared beneath the foliage, moving restlessly from place to place. They wore luminous cloaks, with crowns or tiaras on their heads. Some wore jewelry which seemed to be made of clusters of precious gems, wreaths of golden coins and cloth made of gold and silver. Others wore towering helmets or golden headbands filled with large feathers which waved and glistened, while every object gave off a pale, phosphorescent light. The whole scene seemed to be artificial, like gaudy, tinselly, play-acting.

The clothes worn by the busy crowds matched their headwear. Every kind of lavish garment could be seen. Kings and queens appeared, dressed in the gorgeous robes of coronation. There were groups of the nobility (men and women) also decorated with the clothes seen in the pageantry of kings' courts.

Vast groups of people dressed in fine clothes passed by, and behind them I saw tribal people wearing barbaric ornaments of all kinds. Some wore the ordinary clothes of the day, while others were dressed in ancient costumes. In spite of this variety of dress style, every class of spirits acted with the same pomp and pride and restlessly moving, dazzling brilliance.

Then I heard their voices: bursts of laughter, shouts of revelry, lighthearted amusement, and witty ridicule. There were obscenities, horrible curses, and polished sarcasm. Mixed with these were degrading propositions and backbiting, hollow compliments, and pretended congratulations. The sparkling brilliance of it all disturbed and bewildered me.

I moved forward slowly and warily, as if I were treading on scorpions in the middle of red-hot coals. The trees that waved about me were fiery blasts and their blossoms were the sparkle of relentless flames. Each object caused me agony as I approached it.

The phosphorescent glare surrounding each object burned my eyes. The fruit scorched my hand as I picked it and seared my lips as I tried to eat. The gathered flowers gave off a burning gas with a stinking, noxious odor that caused excruciating pain in my nostrils. The fiery atoms of the atmosphere burned as they wafted past me and the air that moved them was laden with disappointment and misery.

I turned to see if I could find even a single drop of water to quench my thirst. As I did, fountains appeared and small streams flowed amongst the bushes and lay in calm and peaceful pools. However, I soon found that the pools were just another deception, and the spray from the "sparkling" fountains fell like drops of molten lead, making me recoil in horror. The small flowing streams were like liquid metal from a furnace, and the deep, still pools were fiery silver in a glowing crucible, where every atom burns with an intolerable glow.

As I gazed aghast at these awful things, a spirit approached me, and I recognized her. She was someone I had known on earth. Here she looked far more brilliant than she had been in the flesh. Her body, face, eyes and hands seemed to have a metallic luster that changed with every movement and every thought.

"Marietta, we meet again. But," and she paused and gazed at me, "I know that you will not stay here, as I must do. You can see that I am now a disembodied spirit. Everyone who inwardly denies the Savior comes here when they die.

"I can see strange feelings stirring in your heart. I felt the same! When I discovered where I was, I was totally bewildered and filled with anxiety. But I also experienced something that you have not yet known. Inside this brilliant exterior is a deep sorrow that I would love to hide." She went on quickly, "But I must tell you, I must warn you."

She went on earnestly. "My life on earth suddenly came to an end. As I left the world I traveled very quickly in the direction of my strongest desires. Inwardly I had always wanted to be pursued and honored—to be flattered by everyone. I wanted to follow the perverted desires of my proud, rebellious heart. I wanted pleasure without restraint, the freedom to fulfil any passion, to do anything I wanted. I wanted to live in a world where there was no religion, no prayer, no church, and no one to rebuke me when I did wrong. I wanted a place where all my time was spent in fast living, with no one to stop me.

"So I entered the spirit world with these attitudes and went to the place suited to them. I rushed to enjoy the glittering things that you can see and was welcomed straight away, for they could see that I belonged here. They did not welcome you because they could see that your underlying desires are quite different.

"I had a wonderful reception. They rushed to greet me and embrace me, shouting 'Welcome! Welcome!' I was amazed and confused, but nevertheless excited and energized by the atmosphere of the place. I found myself pulsating with a strange and restless power.

"A phosphorescent light was given off by every part of me. It concentrated about my head like a brilliant crown, and reflected on my face, giving it a wild, unearthly glow. As I breathed out, my breath became like a robe that wrapped itself around me, making me look just like all of my companions here. I became aware that some strange force was spreading through my brain, absolutely possessing it.

"So I followed my impulses and flung myself into the attractions around me. I wanted pleasure and I went after it. I partied; I joined the sensuous, wild dancing. I picked the shining fruit. I plunged into the rushing streams and gorged myself with everything that seemed to be delicious and inviting. But when I tasted these things I found they were repulsive and caused me more and more pain. My desires are so unnatural that the very things I crave, I detest, and the things I delight in torture me. It gives me a strange addiction. My appetite is dulled, yet my hunger is not satisfied, and cannot ever be satisfied.

"I crave for everything I see, but when I grasp them they bring only disappointment and agony. Every new experience brings strange fantasy, hallucination, and intoxication. Weird things happen all the time, and they give me more hallucinations and more fears.

"I seem to have become a part of the whole scene here. I cannot stop myself from saying what everyone else is saying. I laugh and philosophize. I scoff, blaspheme, and ridicule. Yet everything I say, no matter how impure, is full of sparkling wit, glowing metaphors, and clever persuasion."

She gestured around her. "The waving trees, the shining fruit, the objects of gold, the moving phantoms, the deceiving waters—such a dazzling picture, but they only mock me. I yearn to satisfy my hunger and thirst, but my desire creates an illusion of cool waters I can never drink, of delicious fruits I can never taste, refreshing air I can never feel, and peaceful sleep I can never enjoy. I am fully aware that

35

these things around me are only delusive fantasies, but they are a cruel and controlling magic that dominates and confuses my mind.

"I am continually attracted to evil. I am the slave of perversion and deception and the evil that controls them. My will is dying, and as it dies so does my hope of mental freedom. Instead I am becoming convinced that I am a fundamental part of this whole revolving fantasy."

She looked at me, her eyes full of despair, and pointed around her. "This place, cut off by that dark cloud, is one great sea of perversion and depravity. Here, you find lust and pride, hatred and greed, ambition and strife, love of self, blasphemies and mad partying, all fanned into a raging fire. If some evil is not the specialty of one spirit, there is always another to provide it. The total effect is the combination of every evil. This is where I live and I am bound by it."

She forced my attention to the groups of people milling around. "These are the ones who exploited the poor, the employers who robbed workers of their wages, others who put heavy burdens on the weary. Those who followed false religions are here, as well as hypocrites, adulterers, and murderers. So too are the suicides; those who were not satisfied with their lives and brought them to an end.

"If people only knew about the dark and awful night that they fall into when they die unprepared, they would make every effort to postpone their death rather than speed up its coming—no matter how great their troubles. They would use their common sense and improve their lives. Earth," she added, "is a place of testing for everyone."

She forced me to walk along a path off to the side. "Do you think life is full of grief on earth? Well, here, no matter where you look, you find many more new reasons for gloom. Is your hope of finding happiness on earth fading? Well, all you will ever know in this place is unceasing, unsatisfied and unholy desire."

She paused, a look of pain spreading across her face.

"Not only that, but your senses here are infinitely more acute. On earth there are many sins that do no more than give your conscience a twinge. But here, those same sins penetrate into the very essence of our existence and the pain becomes a part of us. In addition to that, the awareness of suffering and the ability to suffer are far greater here than they are on earth."

She stopped in front of me and looked me in the eye.

"Marietta, it seems futile to try to describe our deplorable condition here. I often wonder, is there no hope? But I know the answer. How can disharmony live in the middle of harmony? When we were in the body we were often warned about the consequences of our lifestyle. But we loved our own ways better than those which are good for us. Now we have fallen into this fearful place. We have caused our own sorrow."

Her face twisted in pain as she reflected.

"God is just. He is good. We know this state we are in is not the result of a vindictive law of our Creator. Marietta, this misery came about by our breaking the moral law. We should have obeyed it and then we would have been safe. We would have lived in peace and wholeness.

"But sin!" she rasped, "You parent of endless troubles! You insidious enemy of peace and heaven! Why do mortals love your ways?"

At this point she fixed her eyes, wild with despair, upon me. I shrank from her awful glare and the torture revealed in her face. Turning around I noticed that many more of the hopeless beings had gathered around her, struggling to suppress their true feelings as they listened to her describing their sufferings. I was filled with horror and turned to try to escape from her.

This seemed to make her grief even worse and she quickly spoke. "No Marietta, don't leave me. Can't you bear it—even for a short time—to see and hear about the things I am suffering? Stay with me, for I have more to tell you." She spoke even more fervently.

"You are shocked by these scenes, but let me tell you this. Everything you see around you is just the surface of even deeper woes. Marietta, there are no good and happy beings living with us. Everything is dark. Sometimes we dare to hope for redemption, still remembering the story of redeeming love. We ask the question: can that love penetrate this place of gloom and death? Is there any hope that we might be set free from these desires and urges that bind us like chains? Will we ever be released from these burning passions in this wretched world?"

Overcome by her feelings, she began to sob, and she did not speak to me again. Another spirit cried out, "Go away and leave us to our lot. You just being here causes us pain. It reminds us of our lost opportunities and ..."

He stopped and paused for a moment, then continued. "No, don't go. I don't know why but I feel compelled to talk to you. I will tell you what we have learned here about the power of evil and why people are so attracted to it. Listen to me!" He paused again to gather his thoughts.

"When a person is in the body, his spirit is difficult to perceive. It is inside him, invisible. But when he dies and enters this place, that spirit becomes the very basis of his existence. It becomes his whole being. It pervades everything, controls everything and inspires everything.

"People on earth refuse to believe that men and women will suffer for their sins when the spirit leaves the body. They think that the love and goodness of God would never allow this to happen. But evil and suffering certainly do exist in this place. The cause of it is obvious, yet people reject it and even accuse God of evil." He looked at me.

"Violation of God's law always has harmful consequences. It brings death instead of life and perfection. It is sin, the breaking of the law that prevents men and women from becoming what they were meant to be. It is sin that removes them from a life with God.

"This fact is obvious in every aspect of our lives whenever laws are broken. This place is full of the awful results of it."

He lifted his contorted face and cried out in despair.

"Why don't people come to their senses and realize what happens when they sin? Why don't they stop sinning and turn to God to escape these terrible consequences? Marietta, you are obviously not one of us. You will leave here and go back to places of peace. Aah!" he groaned. "We are overwhelmed by madness whenever there is even the mention of peace and love. I am telling you these things because you are going back to earth. Tell those people what you have seen and warn them about the terrible things waiting for those who continue to gratify their wrong desires."

I recoiled in horror at his outburst. The hideous look on his face imprinted itself in my mind forever, but at that moment I was removed from his presence.

I knew that what I had just witnessed was utterly and undeniably real. Those spirits were people I had known on earth! But how they had changed! They had become the embodiment of sorrow and remorse. How I wished they could escape to become pure and be able to join those happy spirits in the Paradise of Peace!

Nine

The Intellectual, the False Teacher, and Heartless Worshipers

I N THAT INSTANT, I found myself in a place of complete blackness. I could see nothing—no sun, no stars, no light. The blackness became more and more intense and closed right around me. I felt I was suffocating. There was no way out! My doom was sealed!

Then I heard a soft and beautiful voice in the distance saying, "Ask Jesus for help. He is the One who gives life."

Hope welled up within me, but in a flash a giant wave of rebellion rose up and fought against it. Immediately I fell even further through an immeasurable depth and came to rest in an abyss inhabited by another group of spirit beings. I soon discovered that these spirits were in an even more terrible situation than those I had just left behind.

First, they gathered around me and praised me for the doubts I had about the divinity of the Son of God. Then a spirit of "giant" intellect came up and spoke confidently to me.

"The religion of the Bible is revered by many who live in darkness and are backward in their thinking. But you, of course, should be able to see that it is just a spiritual farce." Loftily he went on. "The God of the Bible, whom Christians call the Savior of the world, was only a man. So all that religious faith can do is restrict the breadth of human thought. It shackles the noble intellect and hinders the development of the human race.

"Those you have just visited are a class of spirits who have been blinded by the deceptive ideas of religious people on earth." He sneered. "They are totally immature when they arrive here. They still cling to the idea of a possible redemption through Christ! They appear to suffer, but their suffering is only imaginary." A look of supercilious pity swept over his face. "Understanding will reach them before long, and then they will discover the foolishness of their religious learning. At present they still cling to it, in spite of the fact that the better part of their nature has rejected it."

He waved his arms grandly.

"Here, we are free. Our intellect is unrestrained and we understand the magnificence and glory of the peopled universe. We enjoy the rich products of the highest qualities of the mind and are constantly lifting ourselves into ever higher intellectual achievements and the nobility of earthly things. Hah! We don't need the religion of the cross to achieve these things.

"Marietta, we were watching you when the blackness surrounded you a few moments ago. We knew you might pray for help in the name of Jesus because that is how you have been taught. We also heard the voice saying 'Look to Jesus.'" He laughed mockingly. "Did that save you? Of course not! You must realize by now that salvation comes from the natural unfolding of your own being, not by calling on someone's name!"

He looked around and continued. "What can you see here, Marietta? Look at the wonders of this existence and get rid of your ideas about the empty religion of the Bible. This place is known as the Second Sphere. Gathered around you now are great minds from many different places on earth. They have a strength of intellect that would never give in to the force of imaginary religion. They never sang the useless psalms and hymns, the foolish music of the church. What they sing about is nature. Yes, and even more, they are a noble part of it, growing and developing together as one."

At this point the spirit talking to me hesitated and then

41

became agitated. I stared, terrified, as I witnessed a dramatic change. His hazy, nebulous form was shaken by a series of shocks, causing him to writhe and convulse. I could not see where the shocks were coming from, but flashes like broad sheets of ghastly light lit up the cloud-like form surrounding him and he struggled wildly to overcome the power that was on him. He fought with all the strength he could muster, but finally groaned with the bitterness of hopeless despair and gave in to it.

Instantly a vast arena opened up before me. At one glance I could see every imaginable kind of vice, together with every type of human society, government, and tribe. I saw atheists and every kind of religion as well as every form of worship. Even the nominal church-going people were there, those who had worshiped under the message of the cross but with hearts untouched by it.

As I watched, I heard a voice from far above saying, "Marietta, don't be afraid, but study this place of confusion. Here are the self-deceived, those who trust in false philosophy and those who hate God. You will also find the counterfeit Christianity of earth with religious mockery and hypocrisy. You will see human wolves who came dressed in sheep's clothing, which satisfied their greed by exploiting simple and unsuspecting people."

As the voice spoke a weird cacophony of sound fell on my ears.

"Listen! Hear that wild chant! It is coming from the thousands who once sang hymns of worship to the living God without any feeling at all. Listen to that croaking organ. Look, the people are standing up. Watch what they do, and listen to what they are saying."

As I think about what I saw I am profoundly aware of my inability to describe it properly. Only those who saw it could understand its horrific reality. I can only say that every evil scheme that could be found in man was alive and obvious.

Each spirit was like an actor, performing the role he had cultivated on earth. I knew that if these people had any hope of happiness it could only be make-believe and futile. Each one struggled to get some kind of fulfillment from the experience, but the dreadful fantasy of the whole thing recoiled onto them with an inexpressible horror.

As I looked, the choir in the galleries stood and began to sing. The dismal sound of the spectral organ grated on my ears, and note after note of their attempts at singing produced only mocking discords. I pitied them as I saw them sink back in utter despair.

Below the choir sat a congregation, keenly critical of the things presented to them. In a Gothic pulpit in front of them stood a man wearing priestly robes. He was their minister, but he had dishonored the Redeemer by his hypocrisy and pride. His love for God was a pretense, and his behavior had brought true Christian ministry into disrepute. In this dreadful place he represented all who exploit and abuse religious things.

In front of him was an open book. He tried to read from it but failed at every attempt. His voice was shrill and piercing, and his accent hard to understand. His face became distorted and he writhed and agonized in his efforts to read. He tried again and again but with the same result. His frustration increased till he burst out vehemently, cursing his own being and everyone around him. He then began to blaspheme God, blaming Him for every wrong and sorrow. He even tried to gather together all created intellect to curse the Creator of the universe.

His oaths, his manner, and his insatiable passion made him so desperate that I was afraid he might destroy everything around him. But he suddenly gave up, exhausted, and I realized that his strength was limited and, to a large extent, he was under the control of his audience.

One glance at the crowd was enough to know why he was suffering like this. Their faces showed deep hatred and maniacal pleasure as they mocked his efforts. They reveled in fiendish delight at his dreadful agonies. But I was aware that their pleasure was like the relief you feel when you rub a bruise, knowing all the time that when you stop the pain will be much worse.

As he sank back, the look on his face was that of horror beyond description. Ghostly fires flashed around him and he writhed with an inner turmoil as tumultuous as a volcano. His agonies were equal to the worst ideas of the sinner's hell. It reminded me of the words of Jesus, "And throw that worthless servant outside, into the darkness, where there will be weeping and gnashing of teeth....where their worm does not die, and the fire is not quenched" (Matt. 25:30; Mark 9:48).

While he lay there, enveloped in the fires of his own unholy passions, one in his audience stood up and rebuked him.

"You fiend of darkness! You child of hypocrisy! Deceiver! Unrivalled deceiver! You are in the hell reserved for the heartless religious teacher! You can never endure enough punishment! You turned religion and the souls of men into nothing more than a means of making a living. Yes, and for this you were even honored and respected! But you took things easy instead of reaching out to the souls of men and women. You did not seek out ruined hearts, and you never brought them the soul-saving truth of heaven. All you did was tell them what they wanted to hear and so you magnified their delusions. Now you are being tormented, and so you should be!

"Get up, you false teacher in your silk gown! Get up and show us how great your false apostleship is. Speak smooth words to us and lead the choir in their ludicrous travesty of a song. Stop your blasphemy and your curses, and stop wishing you could tear God from His throne." The speaker grated out the words. "Your Maker is just, and you have mocked His majesty. You should have shown the world His glory, and by that light thousands of people should have been led to seek His face."

At this the minister tried to leave, but the speaker continued. "No, you hypocrite! You want to escape but you cannot. Look over this crowd of sufferers and then ask yourself why they are here. Yes, it is true that each of them has sinned and is accountable for their actions. But can you look at them here with a clear conscience, knowing how you have misled them?

"Did you try to lead them to God? No! Instead you wrote learned essays and elaborate Bible expositions. You dressed your sermons with brilliant poetry and marvelous oratory, but the only result was that people were lulled into even greater apathy while you received honor for your clever words."

At this point the former minister cried out, "Stop! Stop! Leave me alone! My remorse tortures me and I have had enough! It never ends! Stop! Don't cut me down! I know I deserve this suffering. I know that all my life I did things just for pleasure. I trifled with men's souls and wrote about eternal things without any conviction. I put my prayers together only to please people. I interpreted the Bible to suit the selfish and fickle and proud, and I found excuses for those who oppressed others.

"This existence is pure horror! Sorrow has gripped me, and endless night! I hear the wailing voices; I see the madness of frustrated spirits. They haunt me! If I try to escape I find multitudes of evils in front of me like ghosts. They give no rest to the souls here. My parishioners drive me mad with their bitter curses. The memories of my secret sins rise up like demons and give me never-ending pain. Spare me a deeper hell!"

As he said these things the whole audience stood up and mocked him in his agony. The spirit who had rebuked him continued to censure him: "You knew very well that we would have done what you told us to do. But when we did wrong things—things that could cause us to end up in this place—you, our supposed teacher of religion, did not try to correct us!

"The Bible, that sacred book, is a gift of God to guide

45

people to heaven! But it was misinterpreted by ministers and theologians like you. You all loved pleasure, your hearts were far from God. Your version of the Bible was a passport to this place!

"Now all we know is bitter grief. Our sins ripen here, and turn into living things. The latest fashions that were once so important to us, bind us now like unquenchable fire. And the money god we all worshiped sits like a ghost in the clouds of death that hang over the abyss."

He shook his finger at the former minister. "Your life here is the consequence of breaking the law of life. You violated it! You were driven by your love of glory! Your kind of religion was hypocritical, like a clean white grave. On the outside you looked beautiful and pure, but on the inside your heart was a den of lust and pride, a lair of snakes' thoughts. It was a tomb full of dead men's bones, the legacy of other bigoted, heartless ministers and theologians.[1]

"Do not curse your Maker," he laughed mockingly. "This is your well-earned reward. Listen and I will quote you a Bible scripture that you so often preached so carelessly. Listen to this!

"'The one who sows to please his sinful nature ... will reap destruction' (Gal. 6:8). Here is another: 'For the wages of sin is death' (Rom 6:23).

"Those verses ring so loudly here now. They reach every home of every spirit. They touch every part of our senses. Worse still, they are magnified to the utmost by the doom of this place.

"No, you false teacher, let God and His word be true, for sin has done this to us.[2] We suffer because we have violated God's law."

As he spoke these words he began to tremble violently. He became more and more agitated until he and the rest of the congregation collapsed on the floor. As this happened, they seemed to lose their individualities and began to blend together into a mass of agitated life. Above this mass rose a thick cloud, so dense that it appeared to be a part of the writhing body below.

The sight was too much for me. I could not endure any more of these woeful scenes. I shrank back and cried, "Isn't there a God of mercy somewhere, and can't He see these things and save these people?"

"Yes," declared a voice above me. "Yes, there is a God of mercy. He sees sinners and yearns for them with the greatest compassion. Haven't you read the scripture that says: "For God so loved the world that he gave his one and only Son, that whoever believes in him shall not perish but have eternal life" (John 3:16)?

The voice took on a grieving tone. "But even though salvation is offered to the whole world, even though Christian believers explain it to sinners and plead with them, there are millions who refuse it. Then there are the millions of others who pretend to believe, but have their own false ideas about redemption. Still others experience grief on earth because of their own sins, but many of these will not change. They fall into terrible misery, simply because they broke the law of purity and love."

I looked up, trying to determine where the voice was coming from. "Don't be afraid, Marietta, but be aware of these things. Realize too that you have seen only a fraction of the suffering that sin brings to the spirits of men and women. Spiritual sufferings are beyond the power of description. Even the things you have just seen cannot give you a full understanding. Let me explain."

The voice continued.

"The spirit of "giant" intellect represents the spirit of antichrist. He tried to confuse you with arguments that seemed reasonable. But behind all of this lay disharmony, love of self, treachery, cruelty, impure desire, lust, rape and murder, the denial of God and His saving mercy, together with sacrilege and blasphemy. He tried to deceive you. He tried to conceal the things that happen to those who are not controlled by God's love. But he failed, and you learned that only Christ can save someone from the effects of sin. All else is futile.

"Then you saw the choir in its gallery, with all kinds of evil. This was only a part of the picture. If you had seen it all it would have been too much for you. This choir represented people of the world singing to whatever god they worship. In their hearts they had no love for the one and only God, and they mocked Him with mere lip service.

"In the pulpit you saw a false teacher and the bitter consequences of hypocrisy in religion. The people in front of him worshipped in the name of the cross but without a true reverence for God. They appeared to be worshipping, but their hearts were far away, trying only to please themselves in their devotions. They chose a teacher who wanted only to receive their accolades, so he tried to satisfy their every whim.

"The spirit who berated him was one who trusted in false teachers and did not care about their own spiritual well-being. The conflict you saw is typical of this kind of people. They blame their sins on each other. This spirit actually acknowledged that justice had been done—that their condition was caused by their breaking God's law. Deep inside, people are aware of their guilt and they know God is good. Those who stop their foolishness and follow God's law can easily understand this.

"You saw the agony of the false teacher as he was told the truth about his past. He showed you what happens to those who gratify their wrong desires on earth. They ultimately meet here again with their old acquaintances and blame each other for their sins, and tell them the truths of God that they should have followed.

"Their final falling and blending into one mass illustrated how sin attracts sin. People with similar characters and desires are attracted to each other. As more of them gather, the dominating forces of sin grow stronger. So each spirit inflicts sorrow on the others and receives sorrow in return.

"The thick cloud above them was the spiritual discord which fills the great area.

"Finally Marietta, this scene demonstrated the verse that says, 'If a blind man leads a blind man, both will fall into a pit' (Matt. 15:14). That is what happened here."

The voice paused and continued solemnly, "Marietta, you have had enough of these things, but do not forget them. Never forget that "the wages of sin is death" (Rom. 6:23).

Ten
_____

Escape From Hell and Lessons Learned

THE VOICE CEASED and I heard an angel say, "Marietta, come up here!" Immediately I was drawn up into a cloud of light, which then rose gently.

The change was incredible. Only a moment before I was watching in fear as a maddened crowd ran wild. Now I was soaring away from it into a glorious brightness.

I mulled over the things I had seen. First I had learned that sin brings death. Secondly, that happiness does not come from disobedience but from simple faith—faith in Jesus as Redeemer. Then I had discovered that deceit is the foundation of darkness and the source of much trouble. It is a camouflage to hide the consequences of lying and evil. In addition to this, I saw very clearly that no deception—no matter how cleverly fabricated—can conceal truth on that final day when everything is tested.

But then a new light burst on me and I turned to see above me an incredibly lovely being. Her clothing was bright as the sun and her face shone with heavenly goodness. She sat calmly and peacefully in the midst of a divine radiance, and spoke to me.

"You can rest here, Marietta. Put aside your thoughts now about the things you have just seen and don't be overcome by them. God has prepared a home in heaven for everyone who is willing. Whoever has a need and seeks God will find He is always there to help. The people you saw now live with the consequences of all they did when they were on earth. It is inevitable. It is like a person who has a big fall. He will hurt himself and must bear the pain. This is the 'law of being.'

"But rest for awhile, Marietta. I can hear angels coming. They are singing songs of praise to our Redeemer. Listen to the beautiful harmonies. Look up, Marietta!" she urged. "Look! We are coming close to a city of righteousness. No evil can enter here, and no false spirit will ever pollute the holy temple in this place. Listen, a guardian angel of the holy hills is talking to you."

I looked up and a voice spoke. "Marietta, where do you want to go now? You left the sinful earth. Why do you want to go to places that are evil? How can you waver between the worlds of good and bad?

"I have been watching you. I saw you in the Paradise of Peace and then I saw you fall into the place of the wicked. I watched you sink under its burden and heard you cry for God's help."

The voice came closer. "Learn from this! Your heart must be grounded in truth and controlled by holy love. If it is not, you are vulnerable to the forces of evil. There is no safety for someone who is not born of God. You are exposed to the forces that can ultimately lead you to outer darkness.

"If you want to follow truth and enter paradise, you have to deny yourself the 'pleasures' of sin. Get rid of things that cripple your desire to follow God. Change your ways and do good. This is the only way you can receive everlasting good.

"Marietta," the voice went on, "you were shown these things for a very important reason. You represent people who have not made up their minds about spiritual issues. Take this lesson back with you: a perverted spirit—such as you have seen—will continue to do evil when left to its own devices. If there is no restraint, that spirit will then aggravate the grief and suffering of the other spirits around it."

The voice paused, and then continued. "It is the same in the world. The increase of sin in the world is simply dependent on the number of people who pursue sin. One evil person will encourage another, and destroy much good. Sin added to sin increases its power, until eventually families, tribes and nations arm themselves for war. If only mortals knew the power of evil!

"Marietta, you could well write the word 'sorrow' over all mankind. So many people multiply the evil in their lives by persisting in sin. And they finally end up in the world of evil spirits, joining many others like themselves."

The voice quickened, "But if the grace of God is allowed to enter a heart, it changes the character and even the desires. Whenever divine life enters a soul it turns the mind toward God. Then, because of the law of holy attraction, it enables that soul to enter paradise.

"Marietta, this city is the one where you saw the infant nurseries. You have seen the places of sorrow and death, now you are allowed to return again.

"We are above the center dome of the infants' nursery now and you can see the educational temple. The schools of Infant Paradise are all here."

As the spirit finished speaking, the great dome below us suddenly opened up, revealing all its glory and magnificence. I saw the grandeur, variety, and order of the entire paradise. At the center was the cross, and around it were the twelve spirits, each holding a smaller cross and a harp. The infants all had their attention fixed on the twelve spirits around the cross. All was silent.

Eleven

The Music of Heaven and the Separation

"LISTEN, MARIETTA," SAID the angel. With her right hand she pressed my temple and from the deep silence I heard music begin. It was like angelic breath, like the inner and most holy life of the spirit. I could hardly hear it, yet it moved softly over and through me. I had never realized there were elements within me that could be awakened to such sacred music. I thought that my nature must have been totally transformed for me to experience such harmony. I felt totally at one with it.

As the sounds continued, it came into my mind to force myself into the music, rather than simply allowing it to flow through me. My willpower wove itself into the sounds, and immediately discord flared up and the full force of my sinful nature swept over me. Note after note continued to penetrate me, but they no longer moved in unison with the musical chords of my inner being. In striving to blend with the music, I had produced a terrible discord. Several cadences broke up in this way, and the music became harsh to me. I knew my nature could never meld with it.

The discord within me became agonizingly painful. Every part of me rasped and grated. The waves of harmony that moved throughout the dome foundered in a sea of turbulent sound when they fell into my degenerate heart. I wanted to get away. Any other thing or any other place would have been better by far. I thought even the hellish place of false worship would fit my nature better. But I could not escape.

I was completely disoriented. Each moment seemed like an eternity, and my condition became more and more awful. Finally I cried out in despair, "Let me get away from this place!"

I tried to analyze what was happening. I loved the sacred music when I first heard it. But when I tried to join myself to it a discord was created and my unholy nature was exposed for all to see! Obviously I was not fit to be with angels. I was lost beyond redemption, my spirit broken and fallen. No part of it was compatible with that place.

I cried out in agony, "Let me get away! Let me hide in darkness forever! Angel! Hide me! Hide me from this light! It has exposed my sinfulness! This harmony is torment! Save me from it! Is there a deeper hell somewhere? Let me go there—even if I am lost and demons mock me. At least my spirit would not be awakened only to be crushed because it is not fit for this place!"

So I pleaded to be released from the light and harmony and peace that filled that place. I realized I was completely unfit for paradise. I had wanted so much to be there, but had not considered what changes were needed in me before I could enter.

It was true that I had seen the deformity of the infant spirit, and watched amazed as it was restored by the grace of God.[1] But I had never applied this knowledge to my own situation.

In addition to that, when I was sucked down by the darkness I had looked up to heaven, passionately wanting to go back there and be saved. Little did I know I could suffer so much agony from the love and harmony of heaven. I had no idea my own condition would cause me misery equal to the deepest hell.

All these thoughts now raced through my mind as I begged for help. My condition was plain to me. I was certain all was lost and I was doomed to bitter grief.

At length the angel spoke. "Marietta, you are not lost. Yes, your sin has been exposed and you are suffering because your spirit has discovered its true state. But perhaps now you will understand how good God is in providing redemption and transformation through the Lord Jesus.

"When you first came here you had no idea of your real position. As a guest you were permitted to receive a covering of holiness which protected you and enabled you to enter. But in this place, the breath of holiness is so perfect that your inner life was penetrated and your sin exposed. That is why you are suffering.

"You can now see why God has arranged for spirits of similar nature to be kept together in the same place, with good and evil kept apart. The misery experienced by the evil is not increased and the happiness of the good is not diminished. This is why the apostle John said that no unclean thing can enter the Holy City.[2]

For no unholy soul can ever enter this sacred temple or this city of inner life. In the same way, the inhabitants of this happy place could not live in the place of darkness with spirits that have not been reconciled to God."

The angel reached forward in earnestness. "Marietta, can you see the goodness of God in this law of existence? It would be unjust of a righteous Creator if He condemned any of these infants to the dark regions. Their pure and tender natures would shudder if they were even touched by the inflamed passions of its inhabitants. Certainly God could be considered unjust if He treated the innocent in this way.

"In the same way it would be unmerciful to send an evil spirit to the place of holiness. For the greater the light and supreme good of that place, the greater would be their suffering."

She leaned back again. "So, you can see that God is wise and good. This is the fulfillment of the Bible verse that says, 'Let him who does wrong continue to do wrong; let him who is vile continue to be vile; let him who does right continue to do right; and let him who is holy continue to be holy' (Rev. 22:11). In other words, let there be a separation between good and evil spirits.

"It is written that there is an impassable gulf fixed between the unholy and the righteous because the two extremes cannot blend.[3] Whoever is born of God is born of love, and love has no similarity to hatred. Whoever is under the dominion of evil does not love God.[4]

She paused for a moment and then spoke again. "If mortals only realized this, they would war against evil and live righteous lives. Marietta, think about the things you have seen. Use your common sense and bring your life into order. Otherwise, a worse thing will happen to you, worse than just the realization that you are not fit for this place. When you return to the world, put your trust in Jesus. He is the only one who can make you fit to return so that you can enjoy the happiness here."

The angel's rebuke struck my heart like an arrow, and I began to cry. "Do not weep, Marietta," the angel continued, "A ransom has been provided to save your life. There is a 'healing fountain' and it will wash away your impurity.[5] So be encouraged! God's mercy is vast, and He offers redemption to everyone who wants to be rescued from their prison and brought into His kingdom. That is why the saints in heaven are always singing hymns of thanksgiving to their Redeemer. Day and night, they never stop!"[6]

On saying this, the angel touched my forehead and a stream of light filled me. I stood up, strengthened and refreshed. "Now," said the angel, "the infants have just been brought into the center dome of instruction from the temples of learning. Listen to their songs."

The infant voices rose up, filling the expanse and swelling into gentle waves in the atmosphere above. They had formed into small groups, which then united to become one. It was a beautiful sight. Each infant seemed to glow with holiness as they sang the sacred songs.

A female spirit was moving from group to group, dressed in pure white clothes and a dazzling crown set with gems on her head. She held an open book in her left hand and a scepter in her right. She listened to each infant carefully, so that she knew how the voice of each one related to the other and also to the whole group. She was watched closely by the infants who sought to follow her example, just as students follow their teachers in schools on earth.

There were many parts to the music but they harmonized as one. As they sang, their fingers moved over their soft, mellow harps with increasing confidence so that they became like one person, with the spirit and harmony of heavenly love.

Twelve

Infant Instruction—the Lost Man

AT THIS POINT a totally different scene was presented to the infants as part of their preparation for advancement. To help you understand what happened next and the reason why these extraordinary scenes were shown to the infants, I need to explain that some of the instruction in the spirit world is given by dramatization.[1] Real-to-life scenes are presented to the infants to teach them about past events or to illustrate important principles.

In this way the spirits can be taught, even when they have no scientific or artistic wisdom, no knowledge of moral or spiritual laws, and no understanding of the complex universe. The "dramatizations" are so clear the infants can easily grasp them and absorb the information presented.

To fully explain everything used in this process, even for that very basic infant school, is simply beyond my ability. It would also require volumes to contain it all, even if it could be written down. As a result I must condense it to a summary form and you must be satisfied with that.

*   *   *   *   *

The light and glory that illuminated the dome gradually dimmed until only a half-light marked the outline of the great city. Everything fell silent and nothing moved. The stillness of that moment was broken only by a gentle breeze wafting across the vast plain.

After a brief pause, a moonlit landscape from earth appeared. Beneath a bank of gloomy clouds was an underground cave, and in this cave lay a man. He was badly wounded, apparently dying, and he tossed to and fro trying to obtain relief. The attention of every spirit was fixed upon him.

His tossing and turning was fitful and convulsive, but completely futile. He tried to heal his wounds by applying what he thought were effective medicines, but they were all unsuccessful. In fact they only increased his suffering and probably added to his peril. The cave where he was lying was surrounded by an abyss, and though he made several attempts to cross it he failed each time, finally giving up in utter despair.

As he lay weak and helpless, a group of people gathered around him—a woman, some teenagers, and children—apparently his wife and family. They were grieving for him and tried to help him. They attempted to bind up his wounds, to lift his head and revive his strength, but to no avail.

As I looked more closely, I saw that he was lying right beside the edge of the abyss. Not only that, but he was being drawn closer each moment by some invisible and irresistible power. It was a moment of great tension. His wife came closer and wrapped her arms around his neck, trying to hold him back. The others tried to help too, but all in vain. He was drawn even closer to the abyss. The effect of his sickness had worsened too, until finally, at the point of death, he lost consciousness. To my surprise, a man who looked like him stood up beside him. I immediately realized it was the spirit of the man, and it had just left his body.

As the spirit stood there, it still seemed connected to the prostrate body and dependent on it, and though it resembled the man it looked far more disfigured and dreadful. Spiritual and moral disease had done its work and I could actually see the results before my eyes.

During this time the body had remained motionless, but the spirit was quite capable of movement and expressed graphically all of his sufferings. He looked up, as if to seek help from above, but a cloud of thick darkness overshadowed him. Then he looked around wildly, seeking some place of refuge or help. But all his efforts were hopeless and he gave up in despair.

Then his gaze dropped vacantly and fell on the abyss, yawning beneath. Convulsing again he tried to escape, but all in vain. The scene was horrible. The agonizing, fruitless efforts, together with the expressions of final despair, showed a complete wretchedness beyond human description.

Then, suddenly, the spirit disappeared and the body showed signs of returning to life. The man recovered, but only to experience great misery in his body again, and to feel his sorry state even more than before.

The little group, however, encouraged by the signs of life, renewed their efforts to restore him, but they had no power to soothe his grief or restore the lost health of his body or spirit.

As they struggled in this way a light descended. Under its penetrating brightness it became immediately obvious that all of the family group were in the same spiritual condition as the man, except that the effect was not as marked. Their final destiny, however, was just as certain. Gradually they became aware of their fate and they cried out for help.

A voice answered out of nowhere, a voice that was somehow familiar to me. "In this situation man cannot help man," it said. "Can the Ethiopian change his skin or the leopard change its spots? (Jer. 13:23). Can the weakness of those who are already dying restore the life of another victim? Help must come from above; otherwise there is no hope at all."

As the scene closed, an angel explained to the infants watching: "This gloomy region you just saw is earth. The people there struggle with many sicknesses—physical, moral, and spiritual—but they cannot save themselves.

"The spirit which rose when his body gave up represents the immortal nature. Even though the body perishes, this immortal nature continues to exist and, in fact, it is even more sensitive in this state. When the spirit sank down in despair it showed you that the effects of moral or spiritual degradation are not cured by death.

"The family group represents human sympathy. People seek help from others in their suffering and this inspires the more benevolent to assist them.

"Those who do this are sensitive to the troubles of others. They deeply sympathize with them, no matter what the cause. They try to remove evil from the world and lift mankind through human efforts. But they have the same inherent weaknesses as the ones they are trying to help, so they can never fully succeed, although superficial relief sometimes inspires hope for a short time. Throughout the ages the human race has struggled with this problem, in countless reformatory measures. Eventually these reformers have given up in despair because of this fundamental weakness in themselves.

"It will always be like this until men and women finally turn to the Lord. He is the only sure stronghold when you are in trouble.

"The voice which declared that man could not help man was the voice of Truth. Truth always tries to show men and women their true condition and to present the truth of salvation through the Lord Jesus."

The angel then turned his attention away from the children and looked up to the higher heavens. His voice was meek but fervent: "Father of all, let your Spirit inspire these young minds with understanding. Let them benefit from what they have seen concerning the effects of sin and the wonders of Your love in Your way of salvation. Support them with Your grace as they now watch the trials of their Redeemer at the hands of those He tried to save.

"Grant that they may be prepared well, so that they can

advance to the heaven of youths where your glory is revealed in even greater love and blessing.

"You have entrusted your angels with the care of these little ones. They delight in leading them higher, so that Your glory may be reflected on them in a way that is pleasing to You. Let Your will be done by these angels so that the spiritual understanding of the children will increase and the love in them be released. In this way Your name will be glorified in them for ever. To us who minister Your grace, You are all and in all."

The guardian angels and instructors responded, "Evermore, amen, evermore, evermore, amen," and the heavenly atmosphere echoed it until the sound finally faded away in the distance.

Thirteen

The Bethlehem Story

T HERE WAS A short pause and then a distant voice said, "You will now learn of the events that took place when God came to earth as a man to change the destiny of your world."

* * * * *

The glory of God lit up the sky, and a choir playing golden lyres sang loudly, "Glory to God in the highest, and on earth peace and goodwill to men. I bring good news! It will give great joy to all the people! 'Today in the town of David a Savior has been born to you; he is Christ the Lord'" (Luke 2:11).

Beneath a pale light the city of Bethlehem came into view. This was the birth place of the Redeemer. What a tremendous contrast it was in comparison to the home of the infants in paradise. These children lived in the glory of divine life, attended by angels, blessed by the Redeemer and greeted by heavenly choirs. In stark contrast, they looked now upon the dreary world surrounding that marvelous event, the birth of Jesus of Nazareth.

Jesus! The untold goodness and love of God was revealed through Him. Yet here He was, a baby in the arms of his lowly mother, Mary. Both the children and the watching angels were deeply moved to witness the humble circumstances of His birth.

After a short pause, an angel said, "This is the birth place of the Redeemer whose glory illuminates this temple. He took this humble form for you, and in so doing has made it possible for you to have homes in heaven, if you trust in His grace and be obedient to the law of redemption. Adore Him for He is worthy!"

"We will adore Him forever," said the chief guardian, and the children echoed, "We will adore Him." Then again, all fell silent.

The scene then focused on Mary. She was resting against Joseph, who held her close to him while she gently cradled the baby in her arms. Standing nearby were a few Israelites, their eyes fixed on the babe and His mother. Around them were countless angels—invisible to human eyes. (See Luke 2:8–20.) They were holding crowns in their hands, but their harps lay at their feet. A cloud of glory rested above them and a voice came from it, saying, "This is my beloved Son." (See Luke 3:22.)

The angel spoke again, "Today, God's love for man is revealed. Man has fallen because of sin, but now salvation has come. You will see Justice and Mercy enter the scene to debate the destiny of fallen men and women. Justice will speak out against sin so that God's righteousness is upheld. On the other hand, Mercy will plead for the sinner who suffers continually because of sin."

"Let us bow down and adore the God of our salvation," said the chief guardian. As the children responded another voice said, "It is good for you to worship at the birth of the Savior. Let all heaven worship in this way."

I was reflecting on the worshippers' devotion, when the chief guardian said, "We will rise now. Look, the next scene is appearing." Lifting her eyes to the higher heaven she continued, "Be our help, Father, so that we may understand what heaven is revealing for our instruction, so that we may know your love and be prepared to do your will forever."

Led by their guardians, every child responded, "Amen."

The Justice-Mercy Conflict

A BRIGHT CLOUD CAME to rest just above the infants' temple. From it there descended a mighty being, all-powerful in strength. His majestic brow was inscribed with the word *Justice* and he carried himself with supreme authority. So great was his power and stature it seemed he only needed to speak one word, and worlds would flee and laws would cease forever.

With purpose in every step, he advanced toward a gloomy valley encircled by huge mountains whose lofty peaks soared far into the blue vault above. As he drew near his goal, a dark cloud moved down the mountains. Terrifying lightning flashed around it, as if electric fountains were pouring from an ocean of fire. Heavy thunder shook the base of the massive hills. There was fire, smoke, and storms as the elements seemed to go mad. The scene was terrible beyond description, but Justice continued to advance and the very lightning seemed to wreathe itself into a crown on his head.

Then the word *Destruction* appeared, written in flaming letters in the lightning, reflected on the clouds and echoed by peals of thunder. Huge tremors shook the earth. At the height of the drama a voice wailed in despair from beneath the cloud at the foot of the mountain.

"Save us! Is there no hope at all?"

Heavy thunder rolled around the mountains.

"No hope."

Justice continued to advance.

"No hope," he repeated, as he raised his mighty hand.

"No hope, no hope," echoed the hoarse voices of the raging elements.

"We are dying without hope," cried the voice, now weaker. "We are dying. Doesn't anyone care?"

In an instant I saw again the pitiful group which had been shown to me earlier. The trembling woman was bent over the prostrate man, as if to screen him from the storm. But as she saw Justice raise his mighty hand she fell back, crying, "We are lost! There is no hope! We will die in the abyss!"

Relentlessly Justice continued his advance as if to cut the forlorn man into pieces and crush him with one blow. The man's trembling hands were now raised in prayer and around him his family had fallen down, helpless and pleading.

"You, man, have continually violated the law. Do you think you can trifle with it and not suffer the consequences? Don't you understand that when you oppose the law, destruction must come upon you? The time has now come."

As the voice of Justice ceased, a great light flashed over the scene and a dazzling cloud rapidly descended. From the cloud another being appeared. Her name was Mercy and her manner was the exact opposite of Justice. She was the embodiment of meekness. She halted Justice, who was still advancing toward the fallen group, and embraced him.

"Why must you be relentless?" she demanded. "Why must this sinner perish? Is there no hope for him?"

In a voice that shook the heavens above, Justice replied, "No hope can come from his fellow man!" Even the stars trembled and the earth quaked and reeled as he spoke. "No hope exists in the fallen world," he repeated, still advancing and poised to strike.

As the blow was about to descend on the sinner, Mercy spoke again. She bent protectively over the bleeding form and placed her left hand on his heart. Holding back the arm of Justice she lifted her face and called out to God.

"Your throne, O God, endures forever. Your Word stands forever.[1] There is no end to your years. You, O God, are holy. The foundation of your throne is righteous. It is the glory of the everlasting hills and the defense and safety of the heaven of heavens where countless tens of thousands of glorified seraphim are gathered.

"Here, O God, is a man, fallen into sin. We know he has taken your rule lightly, violated your law, and challenged your rightful vengeance. He has trifled with your will and fought against eternal and unchangeable justice. He has fallen and lies here dying. Yet, O God, you have created him an immortal and spiritual being. He is also a rational being, and therefore he is accountable. Because of sin he now lies on the brink of the bottomless abyss. If he falls, he will suffer pain and grief forever.

"My name is Mercy, and mercy is an attribute of your throne. Justice and mercy both belong to you, O God! Let your love descend, O Eternal One."

She turned to Justice. "And you, Justice, spare this fallen being! Spare him, even though he has sinned and sold his eternal good for a pittance!"

At this point Mercy bowed her head, waiting for the decision.

A voice from the cloud then said, "Mercy, you have pleaded for the sinner and heaven will listen to you. Justice, delay your execution. Mercy, can you find a ransom for the sinner?"

One of the watching angels cried out the answer: "God loved the world so much that He gave His only Son (John 3:16). He is the righteous one who will pay the ransom and bear their sin." There was a pause and a woman approached. It was Mary, the mother of Jesus. She bent down with Mercy beside the dying man and held the baby towards him as she looked reverently up toward the cloud.

The voice continued from the cloud, "This is my beloved Son. I am well pleased with Him. As it is written, 'A bruised reed he will not break, and a smoldering wick he will not snuff out, till he leads justice to victory. In his name the nations will put their hope' (Matt. 12:20–21)."

Then Justice replied, "Has your Son experienced temptation and conquered it? Has He 'suffered outside the city gate' as it is written of him (Heb. 13:12)?[2] Has He conquered death? Can He hold back the storm of sin and death? Can He change the diseased nature of the heart? Can He descend into the vortex of death and stop that mighty current flowing down to the abyss?"

Mercy stood straight and spoke with a boldness that belied her meek nature. "Here, Justice, is your answer."

The scene changed to the Mount of Olives at Jerusalem. (See Luke 19:37.) There I saw the man Jesus. He lifted His eyes toward heaven and said, "Here I am—it is written about me in the scroll—I have come to do your will, O God" (Heb. 10:7).

As He spoke, a huge multitude of deformed beings appeared before Him. They were afflicted with every possible kind of human suffering and depravity. Addressing them with pity He said, "If anyone is thirsty, let him come to me and drink....I am the way and the truth and the life. No one comes to the Father except through me" (John 7:37; 14:6).

Another voice then spoke. "This is Jesus. He the Son of David, the hope of Israel, the bright Morning Star, and the Sun of Righteousness.[3] He is truth in all its redeeming glory. You, who are perishing, trust in Him! He has come to redeem you."

Again I saw the mangled form of the dying man. He had heard the words but his mind was dull and heavy. He could hardly understand what was being said, but he looked up to see if help was at hand. Jesus, who had been standing on the Mount of Olives, came down and bent over him, saying, "What do you want?"

The man answered, "If only I could be saved!"

Jesus answered him, "That is why I came—to seek and to save what was lost" (Luke 19:10).

Then Justice said to Mercy again, "Where is your ransom?"

"The ransom is Jesus," she responded, "'the Lamb of God, who takes away the sin of the world (John 1:29)!'"

Jesus spoke again, "This is why I came into the world." (See 1 John 3:8.)

"Yes," said an angel, "and by the wounds you received from the lash, the sinner is healed." (See 1 Peter 2:24.)

"But has He won the conflict?" Relentlessly Justice turned to Mercy, and said, "You are pleading the cause of the sinner and have proposed this Jesus as a ransom. Well, understand this: until this 'Redeemer' has fought and won against sin and death, He cannot rescue this fallen man. Do you still want the man's salvation?"

"Yes," answered Mercy. "That is why I am intervening."

The Judas Betrayal

THE SCENE SHIFTED to another location. Please understand that I have found it extremely difficult to describe the following events. My words are totally inadequate.

I saw Jesus seated with a group of His friends around a table. One of them was leaning devotedly against Him and listening to Him. Their eyes were fixed on Him and filled with sorrow as He said, "I tell you the truth, one of you will betray me" (Matt. 26:21).

Then He took some bread, blessed it, and broke it into pieces. He gave it to them and said, "'Take and eat; this is my body.' It is going to be broken for you" (Matt. 26:26).

Then He took the cup of wine, gave thanks to God, and passed it to them, saying, "Drink this, for it represents the blood of the new covenant between God and mankind. My blood will be shed for many for the forgiveness of sins. And I tell you, I will not drink this again until that day when I will drink it anew with you in my Father's Kingdom" (Matt. 26:27–29).

The solemn mood was broken by the thunderous voice of a mighty angel. "'The Son of man will go just as it is written about Him, but woe to that man who betrays Him! 'It would have been better for him if he had never been born'" (Matt. 26:24).

"Woe to that man" came a heavy response, "For it would have been good for him not to have been born. Woe, woe,

woe to that man." Many millions echoed the cry, and the elements shook.

The little group stood up from the table, sang a solemn hymn, and departed. When they left, I saw one of them slip away, silently and unnoticed by the others. As he went, his steps became urgent and his face revealed an inner turmoil that burned with the consuming fires of hatred. I wondered about this. I could not understand what caused such a great change in him so quickly. Only moments before he had been seated with his friends, all of whom were grieving because of what Jesus had just said about His betrayal and afraid that He would leave them.

Jesus was the one they looked to for advice and safety. They had depended on Him and hoped in Him. Now He had told them He was leaving, and when He said one of them would betray Him, they were a picture of misery. I heard them ask with deep anxiety, "Lord, is it me? Lord, is it me?" (See Matthew 26:22.)

He had spoken at length about His coming departure.

"In a little while you will see me no more, but later on you will see me again.[1] I know this causes you grief. But I tell you the truth: it is for your good that I am going away. Unless I go away, the Counselor, the Holy Spirit of God, will not be able to come to you; but if I go, I will send him to you.[2] I won't leave you alone like orphans.[3]

"Do not let your hearts be troubled. Trust in God and also trust in me. There are many rooms in my Father's house. If this were not so, I would have told you. I am going there to prepare a place for you. Then I will come back and take you to be with me, so that you too may be in the same place where I am.[4]

"Before long, the world will see me no more, but you will see me again. Because I will live again, you will also live again.[5] I tell you the truth, you will weep and mourn while the world laughs, but your grief will turn to joy.[6] Right now is your time

72

of grief, but when I see you again you will rejoice, and no one will be able to take away your joy.[7]

"Up until now I have been speaking in pictures and metaphors, but the time will come when I will no longer use this kind of language—I will tell you plainly about my Father."[8]

The little group believed these encouraging words as He foretold His departure, but they were still devastated by the thought of His leaving. They loved Him—and He deserved that love. His words were full of goodness and His actions showed such heavenly love and fatherly care that I wondered what could possibly induce any of them to betray Him.

While I was pondering these things, the angels began to instruct the infants.

"See the contrast of good and evil. Those men who shared the Passover meal with the Lord were His disciples. The Lord knew His time had come and He knew who would betray Him, so He prepared them for the trial and the things that would follow. The one who secretly withdrew was Judas Iscariot, who betrayed His master for thirty pieces of silver.

"Children, watch this scene more closely as it continues, and see the two great principles of good and evil which operate in man in his fallen state. You will see them very clearly as the story unfolds."

Judas then appeared, entering the council chamber where the chief priests and elders of Israel were gathered. They were plotting to capture and kill Jesus and bring scorn and dishonor on him.

But now Judas was a different person! His spirit had changed dramatically since the Last Supper. His face was contorted with rage and his heart was full of malice and treachery.

A pale light lit up over his head, revealing a group of demonic spirits, urging him on. They displayed every facet of the evil nature of their master Satan, that arch fiend, the destroyer of peace. Satan is the instigator of crime, the enemy of all that is good and right, luring the souls of men and women to him. And so these demons poured out their fiendish and hellish temptations, and filled Judas with their hatred for the Son of man.

The priests rose as Judas entered the council chamber. They greeted him with malicious smiles and the chief priest addressed him:

"Welcome Judas. You have shown yourself to be a friend of all that is right—a friend of God's ancient temple and the Law of Moses, and a friend of the people of Israel.

"We want to talk to you about this so-called king of the Jews, this man Jesus. We believe you have been close to Him. He has deserved death for a long time because of His unauthorized teachings. He has sought the destruction of this beloved city of Jerusalem—the city especially favored by God—and even prophesied the destruction of the great temple!" [9]

The priest raised his voice.

"He said He would put down our authority as leaders, change laws and customs, and establish His kingdom on the ruin of Jehovah's kingdom. Hah! He even called himself God! He is a blasphemer against high heaven and mocks the throne of the Eternal!"

The chief priest became more agitated, and his voice quickened as he strode up and down.

"He called us hypocrites and blind leaders of the blind, when it is God Himself, by His own right hand, who has appointed us as teachers in Israel! [10] This fellow acknowledged that we priests have the keys of the kingdom, but He dared to suggest that we deny entry to those who want to enter, because we are 'depraved' and 'love power.'" [11]

His face turned crimson.

"He also said we will not be given eternal life because we love sin. Surely He deserves to die!"

All who were present shook their fists and shouted their agreement.

"He is attracting the gullible and ignorant, and those who

are dissatisfied with the temple," continued the priest. "And by His peculiar ability to work wonders He has been able to deceive many who are worthy of a better calling. Hah! They will soon discover His true character."

He looked sideways at Judas. "It will go well for the first one who exposes Him and enables us to bring Him before the people. The nation will give this person great honor, and lasting blessings will be on his head."

The associate priests all nodded their heads in agreement.

This was enough to inspire Judas to be that person. So he put forward a proposal to deliver his master into the hands of a group organized by the priest. He made only one condition which he appeared to have considered previously. He demanded thirty pieces of silver for his efforts.

It was evening, and I saw Jesus walking slowly with three of His disciples. His face was filled with sadness. They stopped and He said, "I am overwhelmed with grief. Stay here and keep watch with me. Watch with me and pray also so that you will not fall into temptation." [12]

Then He went a little farther and fell on the ground. As He bowed down on the cold earth in the deepest agony He prayed even more earnestly, and His sweat fell to the ground like great drops of blood. [13]

Above Him the heavens opened and many thousands of angels appeared. They veiled their faces as they bent over the garden of Gethsemane. All was mournfully silent, as they observed the sufferings of Christ the Lord, the Divine Man, the one whom the Scriptures describe as "Wonderful, Counselor, Mighty God, Everlasting Father, [and] Prince of Peace" (Isa. 9:6).

A cloud descended and stopped over the Savior. In it were Justice and Mercy, watching the scene below with intense interest.

After a time the Savior prayed, "My Father, if it is possible, may this cup be taken from me. Yet not as I will, but as you will" (Matt. 26:39).

At this, Mercy said to Justice, "Here is the Ransom."

Jesus prayed once more, "My Father, if it is possible, may this cup be taken from me. Yet not as I will, but as you will" (Matt. 26:39). Then a mighty angel descended and stood by Him, strengthening Him. (See Luke 22:43.)

Mercy then said to Justice, "Look, here is the offering."

Standing up, Jesus discovered His disciples asleep. He spoke to them, "Sleep on now and take your rest." Then he turned, "But look, the time has come! The Son of Man has been betrayed into the hands of sinners!" (See Matthew 26:45.)

My guide then spoke to me. "You have just seen Jesus set the supreme example of humility and submission. He has taken on the burden of human trouble because of His love for mankind. By the power of this love they can be lifted out of their degradation and given homes in heaven—homes of righteousness and peace.

"But Marietta, you will now see something different. The next scene will show you just how real is the perversion of the hearts of men and women."

A turbulent cloud appeared below me, dark and heavy and filled with brawling and squabbling forces. Discordant voices rose from it and I heard the excited rabble saying, "Where will we find him? Hurry up Judas! You're the guide! Take us to his hideout. Time is getting on, and our leaders want the outlaw brought to them. He will die."

"Yes, He will die!" clamored the crowd. They hurried toward Jesus and His disciples but were suddenly enveloped in a cloud that hung over their pathway.

In terror I turned to my guide and asked, "Who are these people? Where are they going? Why are they so agitated and aggressive? Who are they talking about?"

"These are soldiers from the Jewish chief priests and elders," she replied. "They have been sent to take revenge on Jesus."

"But what has He done to stir up such feeling?" I exclaimed.

"Many things. He preached that the time of God's favor is here, and He announced His mission to the world.[14] He gave sight to the blind and hearing to the deaf. He healed the sick, raised the dead, comforted the mourner, and instructed the ignorant. He also urged those who reject the mercy of God to recognize the Creator of heaven and earth as their sovereign, rightful Lawgiver, heavenly Father, and Redeemer."

"And this is why they want to kill him?" I asked in disbelief. "Surely he must have quarreled with them."

She answered, "Haven't you read in the Bible the words of the prophet Isaiah, concerning Jesus? He wrote: 'Here is my servant whom I have chosen, the one I love, in whom I delight; I will put my Spirit on him, and he will proclaim justice to the nations. He will not quarrel or cry out' (Matt. 12:18–19). So He will not enter into conflict with them. Jesus is God revealed in the flesh, but the people are trying to kill Him as if He were a worthless outlaw."

Even as the angel spoke, the soldiers armed with swords and clubs and led by Judas Iscariot, approached Jesus and His disciples. Above Judas I saw a mighty angel of darkness. From it came a pale, sulphurous flame that encompassed Judas and burned in his nerves like fire.

With wild determination Judas advanced and greeted Jesus with a kiss.

But Jesus appeared to be fully aware of his treachery and said to him, "Why have you come, friend?"

Then, turning to the mob, He said, "Am I leading a rebellion, that you have come out with swords and clubs to capture me? Every day I sat in the temple courts teaching, and you did not arrest me" (Matt. 26:55). He gestured toward His disciples. "Let these others go. I am the one you are looking for. This is why I came into the world." (See John 18:8.)

One of the crowd called out, "What do you mean, 'This is why you came into the world'?"

Jesus answered, "I came so that salvation might be given to

the world and that everyone, even those who are hostile and those who attack me, might obtain forgiveness and eternal life through faith and repentance. I will surrender myself into your hands, but you will bring no harm to these disciples of mine."

One in the crowd mocked Him, "You are our prisoner! We are going to take you before the people's tribunal and no one will be able to help you there. How can you say: 'No harm shall come upon these disciples of yours'?"

At this point the disciples turned and ran away, leaving Him in the hands of the soldiers. Then they led Jesus away to the judgment hall.

One of the disciples followed them at a distance.

Sixteen

Jesus the Ransom Must Suffer

AS THIS DREADFUL scene closed, I turned to look at the angelic spectators and children. They now seemed to be more emotionally affected than at any other time. I asked, "How is it possible that there can be sorrow in a place like heaven? Do angels weep?"

Then a voice said, "That is a good question, Marietta. But angels have hearts to feel, and who in heaven could witness the betrayal of the Savior of sinners and not be sad?"

Ten thousand voices responded, all crying out at once, and I strained to hear at least some of them.

"Yes! Who could be unmoved at this sight?"

"Look at the innocent sufferer."

"Look! They are beating Him as they run along."

"They are mocking Him."

"They are laughing at Him."

"They are so cruel!"

"Wake up and look! The people hate Jesus! They are rejecting Him!" (See Isaiah 53:3.)

As the voices ceased, I heard another call, "Look, angels from the highest heavens are coming down."

Far above the crowd I saw a vast company of angels. They had palm branches in their hands and crowns on their heads. As they drew near, a dazzling light preceded them, filling the whole area. So brilliant was its power that even the angels of the highest order in the audience could not look directly at it. I tried to hide myself because it revealed all my imperfections, but nothing could be hidden in that holy light. I wanted to run, but could not. I thought to myself, if this is only a taste of what the highest heavens are like, what hope do sinful men and women have of going there? It would be a consuming fire.

Absorbed in the implications of this thought, I only gradually became aware that one of the cherubic beings was speaking.

"Angels, kindred spirits, inhabitants of the exalted heavens! Bow down before your Lord, for He is worthy. Adore Him from the deepest parts of your spirits. For look! All angels love to give praises to Him! He is worthy of all adoration! Praise Him! Praise the Lord, the Redeemer of earth! While these evil men mock Him and pretend to hail him as King, let us be moved with reverence, and truly worship Him."

Each one bowed down in silent adoration, while the men hurried Jesus to the judgment hall.

As the angels declared him to be God revealed in the flesh, I wondered even more why He did not use His divine power to put down those who were trying to kill Him. I wondered also about the myriads of angels. Any single one of them could destroy at will those who led the Lord away. Why didn't they do something?

Reading my thoughts, the instructor said, "He came to seek and save, not to destroy. He is enduring the scoffing of these evil people so that He can become the ransom for sinners. In this way He is fulfilling the Bible prophecy which says, 'A bruised reed he will not break, and a smoldering wick he will not snuff out' (Matt. 12:20)—meaning that He will not harm helpless people and He will not extinguish the life of man. His mission is one of redemption, not of judgment and execution."

Then I heard voices calling out. They sounded like the roar of many waters. "Be in awe, you earth! For even though your sins have brought you massive condemnation, your Redeemer is offering His life for you. Understand the mighty weight of the burden He carries."

Mercy spoke to Justice, "As it is written, 'For God so loved the world that he gave his one and only Son' to be a ransom for mankind (John 3:16). Jesus is that Ransom. Jesus has brought hope to the world. Sin can now be removed and mankind be at peace once again with God."

Then the angel said to the children, "This is your Redeemer. His life is the only one which can save mankind. You were brought into this paradise because of Him. Watch again now so that you will be able to truly know what the Redeemer has done for you."

Then, with one accord all who were watching spoke out, "How can we ever give enough praise and thanks to God for this gift of life through his Son?"

But, agonizing over their inability to help as the suffering of Jesus continued, the angelic hosts cried out, "Can't we help Him or share His suffering? Look! His enemies are all around Him. They don't know who He really is and they are hurting Him. How can we endure this? Let us help Him!"

The children spoke up, too, "He is our Redeemer!"

One of the mighty angels spoke out, "He is our Lord. His perfection makes the heavens harmonious. All of the heavens declare His name. Yet He is being forced to the Sanhedrin by fallen beings, by leaders of a heartless place where Jehovah is named but not truly worshipped."

Then with one voice they rose up, "Let us beat back these mockers of the Lord."

"No!"

Justice stood in a cloud of intense brightness. In his right hand he held the seven thunders, lightning and storms bursting from them. They spanned the globe like an awful cloud, enveloping the human race, great and small, the living and the dead. They shook the foundations of the earth and made men and women tremble in fear. In his left hand was a scroll containing the law relating to mankind.

Before him was the deformed man pictured earlier, wounded and near death. The blood from his wounds stained the earth where he lay.

Once again Justice answered the crowd. "No! The soul that sins must die. When the law is violated the consequences cannot be changed." (See Ezekiel 18:4.)

At this, Mercy advanced and entered the storm. She bent over the wounded man as she had done before, then straightened and addressed Justice. "Look! He who was, and is, and is to come, has come down to earth. By becoming a man He is able to identify with all mankind. This will enable Him to rescue them from their fallen condition and reconcile them to the eternal law." (See Revelation 4:8.)

"Here," Mercy repeated again, "see the Ransom."

"Yes," said Justice, "the Offering is presented. But it is written that He must do this alone. These", he turned to the angelic hosts, "want to rescue Him and prevent the outcome." (See Isaiah 63:3.)

Mercy's considered response astonished the watching millions. "You are right. It is necessary for Christ to suffer alone in this way."

She turned to the silent viewers. "As the conflict intensifies now, you may watch but you must not intervene. You will see how sin affects man's ability to know what is right. And you will watch the Son of Man fight the powers of death."

But the multitude cried out, "Please, we don't want to see this. We cannot endure it!"

Justice raised his voice, "No! Shouldn't the heavens behold and wonder? Shouldn't Hades quail at the tread of the God-Man as He enters the death-gate to conquer death and bring life and immortality?"

At this, all who were watching became quiet and submitted to him. "O God, let your will be done, in heaven and earth, now and evermore. Amen."

"Let all heaven agree," said Justice, "so that God will be all and over all, now, in the future, and forever."

"Amen! Hallelujah! Hallelujah! Amen!" the multitude resounded. "Your will be done evermore! Amen!"

Seventeen

Apollyon

A S THE VOICES faded, the conspiracy against Jesus continued.

A demon of gigantic size rose up from a smoking pit and towered above the crowd. On its head were many horns from which came lurid flames. A cloud formed from them and enveloped the area, creating an atmosphere of seductive but fiendish hatred.

Upon his forehead was written: *Crucify Him, crucify Him—He does not deserve to live. He seduces the people.*

On his chest were the words: *Apollyon, the Expression of Evil against Good.*[1]

On his heart, in blazing letters I read the words:

Jesus will not win,
But death will consign Him to the tomb
Where mortals sleep.
He has called Himself the Son of God
And made Himself equal with God!
In the tomb He will feel the death shackles
Of my irrevocable decree.
Then I will dash His followers
On the rocks of human prejudice.
For the rest of time they will know
Only gloom, oppression and dismay.

"Hear this!" said a tomb-like voice.

"Hear this!" hissed ten thousand, snake-tongued, demonic faces.

The vault below quivered, as if some mighty ruler of a lower region had touched the deep with his blazing scepter. Then a flame billowed out of the pit. The people in the crowd could not see it but it rose among them and surrounded them. Then, as each person joined the uprising, the intensity of the fire increased, until the whole crowd became like a burning destructive storm. It swept the whole gathering along like puppets, to carry out the merciless and demonic scheme against Jesus.

"The battle is intensifying," said an angel.

He was standing above the storm, in an atmosphere of heavenly holiness. "Death and hell are now joining forces. The powers of evil are falling upon the God-Man, as He takes on the weight of the sins and sorrows of mankind."

Another voice cut in.

"Who will win this conflict? There are thousands of the servants of evil gathered here, and the people around Jesus are becoming just like the demons that are driving them."

They led Jesus into the judgment hall of the Sanhedrin. On His head was a plaited crown of thorns. His temples were pierced, and blood ran down His cheeks. His hands were tied, but He merely looked upward and began silently moving His lips.

At this the host from the pit fell back, as if struck by a mighty hand. They cried out, "Look out! He's speaking with God! He's showing pity! It's not fair! We fight with hate and revenge, and He comes back with love and submission. This is the deepest hell! We have to get away!"

Gigantic Apollyon appeared again. He stretched out his hand, and from it came a dark mass of consuming forces. In a terrible voice he confronted his demons.

"Get up! Enter the combat now!"

His face contorted with fury as he roared at them.

"What is your problem? So what if He looks on His tormentors with love? I can turn hearts of love into hate! I can turn prayers into blasphemies! By my own hand, I will win immortal victory for myself today!"

With that he prompted a man to walk up to Jesus and strike Jesus with the palm of his hand. As he did I heard a movement that sounded as though the heavens above had fallen. I looked up to see all the angels on their knees, their heads bowed and their hands raised. heaven was in mourning.

Another man approached Jesus.

"Are you the Christ? Are you the King of the Jews?" he asked.

Jesus answered, "You are saying so." (See Luke 23:3.)

At the sound of His voice the power of darkness retreated and all was silent.

An angel then spoke to the children in their grief, "Your Redeemer has been struck by an agent of hell, and His forehead has been pierced by a crown of thorns. Evil always tries to strike down anything that is good. These evil beings have come from below to torment men and women. They are full of lust, but cannot express it in themselves, so they try to express it through men and women.

"Satan is trying to destroy Jesus because He plans to rescue people from these evil spirits. More than that, Jesus' mission as Redeemer is to break the power of Satan himself and to crush his kingdom among men. So the evil one is trying to destroy Him and shatter the kingdom of peace, which Jesus is to establish on earth.

"So it is that the two principles, good and evil, confront each other here. Death and hell have come up from the lower realms with raging fires of pride and hatred. They know that the time has come. They have entered the conflict inspired by the deceiver Satan. The battleground is the world because that is where men and women are susceptible to the forces of good and evil."

86

Justice then took up the explanation.

"Not only that, but men and women are moral beings—rational and responsible for their actions. So they stand condemned because of the sin in their lives. God's righteousness speaks out against them. For mankind to live, justice must somehow be satisfied. The human race will perish unless there is a mediator between them and the violated law. This is why a ransom has to be offered.

"Mercy has claimed that this Ransom can enter the great vortex of human degradation and stand among the forces of good and evil to rescue the sinner. This can only be done by reversing the influence of sin that drives man to destruction.

"This is not the only thing that must be done. Evil spirits are able to apply the powers of death and hell onto the deadly effects of sin. So death and hell must also be mastered by the Conqueror, and sin must be bound."

Justice went on.

"Mercy has pleaded for the lives of sinners and so has presented a Ransom. She says God Himself has given help through Him. She says He is mighty and well able to save men and women from their sin. So watch! The Ransom is descending the vortex. If He can, He will defeat death, hell and the grave. However, in the process He must not resist or cry out and He must not complain."

Mercy replied, "He is being led like a lamb to the slaughter, and just as a sheep before its shearers is silent, so He does not open His mouth." (See Isaiah 53:7.)

"Also," said Justice, "He must give up His life as a guilt offering "before his offspring can be saved." (See Isaiah 53:10.)

Mercy's voice rang out again with conviction, "Even though He is descending the vortex of death He will live, and He will live forever. The work of redemption will succeed in His hands. His kingdom will be an everlasting kingdom and there shall be no end to His government. Through this, God's justice will be satisfied and salvation and righteousness will be given to those who believe."

"So be it!" replied Justice.

"Hallelujah, so be it!" echoed the response from spirits, angels, and seraphim.

Jesus called out to a man in the crowd. He was the one who at His arrest had asked why He had come into the world. "This is why I came into the world!" Jesus now said to him, "So that the world might be saved. Since no man can come to the Father except by me, I am now submitting myself to whatever happens to me as a consequence of my mission." (See John 14:6.)

With great emotion, Mercy lifted her eyes to heaven and said, "O God, how great is your goodness. The Redeemer has entered the dominion of death to rescue sinners." Then, approaching Justice, she extended her hand and said, "Is this Offering sufficient? Do you accept it?"

At this, the dying man appeared once again, and Justice leaned over his form. He took the extended hand of Mercy and said, "When the Offering has completed His mission, then the sinner will be restored. He will obtain this through repentance toward God and faith in the Lord Jesus."

Eighteen

The Dream of Pilate's Wife

THE SCENE CHANGED and I saw a company of angels descending from far above. They seemed to be on an urgent mission of mercy. Proceeding to a palace in the city, they paused above it before one of them entered a room where I saw a woman of great beauty. She had been thinking about the events surrounding the arrest of Jesus and was deeply disturbed by them.

She could not see the angel, but it began to soothe her and quiet her nervousness, inducing a soft and gentle sleep. I was intrigued to see how quickly she became quiet and peaceful under the influence of the angel. She rested as the angel breathed on her.

After a time she awoke in the spirit and dreamed that she had entered paradise. She stood by a gently flowing river with beautiful flowers on each bank. The waters of the river were bright and clear and reflected the beauty of the surrounding landscapes. Birds sang softly in the trees and flew above the flower covered plains.

Captivated with delight she raised her eyes and saw countless companies of angels. They had just been singing a great anthem and the echoing melody filled the skies. She stood enraptured for some time, but gradually became aware that their song, and the melody of the thousands of birds, had ended. A death-like stillness gripped the whole realm.

She looked around to see what had caused this and noticed that gloom now obscured the river. The flowers had folded shut. The forests stood still. Not a leaf moved. Even the breezes had completely died away.

The angelic hosts above had veiled their faces, and a weak, pale light now took the place of the bright glory that had shone previously.

Her heart became faint, her face pale, and her eyes dull. Her hands fell lifelessly by her side. It seemed that she was dying but an angel touched her, saying, "Why are you disturbed? Aren't you from the city of Jerusalem, on earth?"

Startled by the voice of the angel she turned to run away, but the angel said, "Don't be afraid. No harm will come upon you in this place. I am a messenger. I came from the large company of angels you saw above you to explain what you have just seen.

"You have been experiencing the glory and harmony of paradise. All those who are pure and blessed, live like this forever. Never-ending praise flows from all these rivers, fountains, flowers, and from all living beings. But then it all changed suddenly, and you want to know why. Listen to me.

"All of paradise is suffering with our Lord Jesus who is being accused today before a depraved and vindictive tribunal. He is God in the flesh, but the Jews want to crucify Him. However, it is necessary for Him to die. This has been written of Him. But woe to those who accuse Him!

"You have a vital interest in this. Pilate, your husband, knows Jesus is innocent, but because of the demands of the crowd he has been pressured into bartering with Jesus' innocent blood. Go to him quickly! Warn him of his danger in opposing the Lord God! Tell him what you have seen. Tell him that while Jesus stands before this demonic tribunal, every tree, plant, and flower in this place is bowed in sorrow and that all heaven waits in awful suspense. Tell him that angels have put down their crowns and dropped their lyres, their voices silent. Go!

Do not wait, or a moment lost may doom Pilate. You must try to save him from any part in this."

The angel who had soothed her into sleep then said, "Wake up!" Startled and terrified by her vision, she got up immediately and rushed to her husband.

"Have nothing to do with that righteous man," she said, "For I have suffered many things in a dream today because of him." (See Matthew 27:19.)

But Pilate disregarded her pleas and gave in to the demands of the people, condemning Jesus to the cross. He gave the order for Him to be whipped and then crucified.

So the sentence was passed, and Jesus was led away.

The Way of the Cross

THE VEIL THAT had briefly hidden the demonic spirits from our view was removed and once again the arch demon Apollyon and his hosts could be seen. He lifted his hand and a massive sheet of sulphurous flame blazed from it like a banner. On it were written the words:

> Victory to Apollyon.
> Today I am victorious over these men.
> They have condemned the innocent.

Ten thousand hoarse, sepulchral voices chanted.

"Hail, Prince of Darkness, all hail! You are victorious. Men and women will feel the sting of death. Go up to victory! Go up! Now we shall rise up from below to witness the God-Man as He writhes beneath the scorpion lash and agonizes on the Roman cross."

"Ah-ha, ah-ha!" came the swelling volumes from the haunts of demons below. The air was rent with loud applause, which swelled and joined with the hellish chant of the mad crowd.

Then a voice cried out in deep anguish.

"Hasn't this gone far enough? Justice, are you totally unbending? Isn't the Ransom complete? Do we have to endure this any longer? He is innocent. Does He have to suffer further? Please spare Him! Look, His back is torn with lashes and

His temples are bleeding! His whole body is shaking! Does the power of evil have to win?"

Justice answered, "He is taking on the suffering of the fallen race and must endure it until the appointed time. But you must understand that His life is not being taken from Him against His will—He himself is giving it up. Satan and evil will triumph for a time, but Jesus will enter the house of this strong man and plunder him." (See Matthew 12:29.)

Again Jesus appeared before us. His body was disfigured, and He was weak and faint. In spite of this they placed the huge cross upon His mangled back and forced Him along toward the place of execution amidst the shouts, jeers, and blasphemies of the people.

Until this time I had been silent, awed by what I had seen. But as Jesus reeled beneath His load, while His body bled from the cruel lashes and His temples were gored and swollen from the crown of thorns, and as I heard the mad cry, "Away with Him, crucify Him, crucify Him!" I could endure it no longer. I cried out to my guide, "Why won't Justice spare Him? Just let the guilty people suffer! They are the ones who violated the law. Let them live with the results! Don't let this continue! Jesus should not have to bear the cross! He is only seeking to save them!"

But nothing changed. Jesus still stumbled slowly along, not speaking but looking on His tormentors with love and pity. He moved more and more unsteadily, until at last His strength gave out and He collapsed, lying still beneath His burden. For the first time His persecutors and crucifiers paused in their cruelty and showed some concern for Him. Perhaps their "concern" was because they felt they might not be able to enjoy His protracted suffering on the cross.

Jesus' collapse had a profound effect on angels and children alike, and they instantly rose to try to help Him. But a distant voice halted them: "Stop! It is written of Him that he shall tread the winepress alone. You cannot help Him." (See Isaiah 63:3.)

"That is right," added Justice, "but let all heaven and earth know that He willingly submits to this suffering for the sake of sinners. It is by His wounds that they are healed. He must now enter the gate of death in order to rescue those who have fallen because of their sin." (See 1 Peter 2:24.)

Mercy then appeared above the cross. "Yes! He has offered Himself for sinners. Justice, here is the Offering I bring."

Justice replied, "You have seen His suffering, but know this! He suffers at the hands of those He came to rescue and not from any vindictive wrath of the Father. So you cannot speak against the goodness of the Lord Creator. This suffering has happened because of Jesus' mission to rescue the heart of man. It is the nature of sin to oppose and try to destroy the good Jesus is doing. Sin is simply being revealed for what it really is."

He continued, "If it was left uncontrolled, sin would make the heavens a place of lawless violence. It would shatter the government of the Lord Creator. It would demolish God's throne and condemn eternal things to hell. Sin is the opposite of good. It is a fountain of evil intentions. This is why, when Jesus came to rescue sinners, the evil in them drove them to torture and destroy Him.

"Jesus wants to save men's souls. Demons want to destroy them. Jesus entered the world as man's Redeemer. Apollyon came as destroyer. There can be no union between these two principles, and that is why Jesus is suffering. It is not by heaven's decree, but because of Jesus' goodness and His plan to save the sinner. This is the reason He is entering the arena of combat with death and hell."

"And will He succeed?" asked an angel who had been listening to Justice.

"Yes," replied Mercy. "He is the Lion of the tribe of Judah; He is the bright Morning Star. He will succeed!" (See Genesis 49:9 and Revelation 5:5.)

"Alleluia! He will succeed!" cried the many thousands

gathered there. "His kingdom shall come and His will shall be done." (See Matthew 6:10.)

"So shall it be," said Justice.

Silence reigned once more. Nothing moved. Nothing disturbed that tense atmosphere while Justice and Mercy paused. It seemed that all who witnessed the scene, even earth's wicked men and the evil spirits from below, had felt the innocence of Jesus. No fault could be found in Him—in His life, during His betrayal, or when He was condemned to the cross. During His life He had healed the sick, raised the dead and cast out evil spirits, bringing untold peace and happiness to the afflicted. He had comforted the brokenhearted, forgiven sinners, rebuked the morally depraved, and cleansed the temple of money changers. When He was opposed and persecuted He had not abused His opponents, but revealed to all a nature that could only be divine.

When the cross was laid on His bleeding shoulders He had accepted it and carried it along in the midst of gleeful shouts and bitter taunts. He endured the greatest humiliation as well as terrible physical pain, and when He fell exhausted beneath the cross He simply looked on His tormentors with compassion and pity.

How could those onlookers fail to sympathize with Him? How could they not shed many tears? How could they refrain from adoring one so worthy?

Finally the soldiers commanded Jesus to get up and continue on to Calvary. Obedient, He struggled beneath the cross, but His trembling limbs failed and He sank again in His agony, struggling convulsively to lift the cross again. Blood from His wounded body stained the ground. The ripped and hanging flesh quivered at the repeated strokes of the lash by the strong hand of the scourger. His "appearance was so disfigured beyond that of any man and his form marred beyond human likeness" (Isa. 52:14). Blood and tears concealed His eyes of love. His lips moved deliberately, speaking words of love and pity: "Sinner, I willingly suffer for you. I endure these things for you, so that you can be saved."

After repeated futile efforts to force Jesus to carry the cross alone, the soldiers ordered a man called Simon, from Cyrene, to carry it for him. (See Luke 23:26.)

As they continued again toward Calvary, a group of women approached the priests who had led the terrible action against Jesus. They bowed before them, raised their hands and earnestly pleaded for Jesus' release. Their sorrow was great, their cause just, their request humble and urgent. But all to no avail.

"He will die," said the priests, and the crowds shouted again, "Crucify Him! Crucify Him! Test Him! If He is really the Son of God, let Him save Himself from the cross! That will reveal His foolishness and blasphemy!"

The Thirty Pieces of Silver

THE SCENE CHANGED again and the Jewish Sanhedrin was before us. As religious leaders of the people, they showed nothing of the humility and servanthood you would expect from such a high office. They were proud and overbearing, ridiculing the solemn issues at hand. They reveled in their triumph of "truth over error", and of "common sense over fanaticism," and congratulated themselves on the prompt and efficient steps they had taken to put down the "impostor" Jesus.

While they were celebrating, Judas rushed in shouting wildly, "I have sinned! I have betrayed innocent blood."

"What is that to us?" they scoffed back at him. "That is your own business."

Taken aback, Judas cried out, "You promised honor and friendship to the one who led you to Jesus. Didn't I do that and give Him to the soldiers? I betrayed my innocent master for you. What is more, it was for your sakes that I sealed my treachery with a kiss!"

He looked down in remorse, then spoke more slowly. "When I betrayed Him, He just looked at me in love. I can't forget that look. I can still feel its power. I have betrayed innocent blood."

He flung down the silver. "You can have it back! I don't want it! It's the price of my Lord! It has cost me my peace forever!"

A priest considered the silver scattered on the ground before them. "Yes, that is the price we paid for your services. But we don't want it either. It is yours. We have no more need of you. Get out before you suffer his fate as well. It seems that you consider this outlaw Jesus to be king. Get out or we will have the guard take you to Calvary too." (See Matthew 27:3–10.)

At this point, a mighty angel drew near to the children and said, "Did you notice how the men behaved here? Their hearts are hostile to God so they sought their own welfare, ignoring the needs of others.[1] Earth's history tells us the same thing over and over. It is witnessed in the tears of servants, slaves, and the oppressed. You will find it in the writings of philosophers, poets, and the wise. They all say it—man is depraved!

"Look at Judas again! He betrayed his Lord. He traded justice and goodness for money. He showed that he had the same depraved and unholy desires as the rest of mankind, only to a greater degree. He sacrificed his greater good, his best friend, for gain. Men will often do this. They trade friendships and abandon their brothers. Even though some of earth's philosophers would like to hide it, too often a man will betray his friend for personal gain. Whose painted walls and costly curtains are not tinged with blood? Whose luxuries may not be traced to the sacrifice of fallen, helpless friends?"

Then another angel approached and said, "Make these truths plain so that the children can understand clearly."

Immediately a series of scenes from earth passed before us. We saw brothers betraying brothers for personal gain, parents betraying children, husbands betraying their wives, and friends exchanging each other as mere commodities. Nation betrayed nation in piracy and war, devastating the poor and helpless. As a result, multitudes of human beings could be seen suffering in the lowest degradation, living and dying without hope. Mothers convulsively pressed their dying babies for the last time to their breasts. Husbands looked on in despair at their maltreated wives and heartbroken children. Poverty, oppression, pain, anguish, rape, and murder were all revealed.

In the midst of these scenes there were a few people who tried to help the oppressed. They tried to take the whip from the scourger, feed the hungry, clothe the naked, comfort the brokenhearted, change war into peace, cultivate true friendship, introduce true religion, enlighten the bigoted, and prevent persecution. They tried to establish universal freedom and peace, founded on justice and mercy. Their efforts were limited, but they did not give up.

Then a light shone down from above, revealing a guardian angel over each one of those involved in this rescue work. Appointed by heaven and full of the Holy Spirit, the angel encouraged and inspired them in their work. As this took place, another light filled the heart of each rescuer who was serving in the name of the cross.

"This light is the Spirit of God," the angel explained. "He inspires all who are born of God so they may work continually to rescue people from sin and its misery and bring them to heaven.

"However, to redeem man requires goodness far beyond human understanding. Only God can do it, because He is love and He is all powerful."

The attending angels then responded. "Yes, we adore God for revealing His love to man. We praise Him for giving help through Jesus who is mighty and well able to save. We will praise Him forever. Yes, forever! Amen!"

At this point the chief guardian spoke, "It's time for you children to rest. Relax together for a while."

Then, addressing a company of spirits at the right, the angel said, "Bring flowers from the holy plains and let their fragrance refresh the young spirits. Spirit of holy quiet, fill them with your everlasting peace."

It was such a good idea to introduce that activity. The minds of the children had been highly exercised by the cataclysmic events, and they needed to be quiet and absorb what they had seen.

After some time had passed a voice spoke, "Who could fail to praise God for His existence, for immortality, and for the joy of paradise?"

The children responded, lifting their hands.

"We will adore our heavenly Father. We will always speak the name of our Redeemer with love and reverence. We will cheerfully follow our guardian angels. And when we are ready we will go out as servants of goodness, wherever the Lord our Redeemer directs us."

Then each guardian gathered her group together and all were ready to continue.

Twenty-One

Calvary

A VOICE SPOKE FROM a cloud far above.

"Prepare to witness the last struggle of the Redeemer as He meets the destroyer in death. Let the sun be darkened and the stars be hidden. Let nature pause and heaven be silent. You seraphim and cherubim, lay down your musical instruments. You flowers, droop your heads; trees, hang down your leaves. Stand still, you waters; breezes be still. You birds, do not sing—while the Redeemer is suffering."

Gradually the darkened mountain of Calvary appeared, etched in pale shadows. In the center stood three crosses on which were hanging human forms. A hushed crowd of people had gathered, and near them was a band of soldiers who had been gambling. But they too were now motionless, disturbed by the strange darkness.

Mournful, wailing cries could be heard from far off. They seemed to stifle the very spirit of life all around. A look of gloom, of utter despair, was visible on the face of every watching spirit.

Eventually, a low whisper passed from angel to angel, murmuring, "Listen! Even nature is suffering! Can you hear that solemn requiem?"

Then all became still again. Not a sound or movement disturbed the silent gloom.

Gradually a pale light began to shine over Calvary. The

three crosses became more and more distinct until the features of the three sufferers could be clearly seen.

"It is Jesus! Jesus is suffering! Jesus is dying!"

The words exploded from every spirit. A sudden shuddering seized them and they bowed their faces, still repeating, "Jesus is suffering, Jesus is dying!"

As they spoke a great cry burst from Jesus' lips.

"Father forgive them, for they do not know what they are doing" (Luke 23:34).

The spirits were completely awed. "Oh what love, what wonderful goodness!" they exclaimed. "He is praying for those who crucified Him! O Supreme Father, give us that same spirit forever."

The soldiers and rulers shouted over Jesus' voice: "He saved others, let him save himself if he is the Christ of God, the Chosen One" (Luke 23:35). This made the spirits lift their heads and stare at the scene in profound grief.

Near the cross a few of the friends of Jesus were standing. They were past weeping. Agony gripped them as death grips a pale corpse. In one of the little groups was Mary, the mother of Jesus. She seemed to be resigned to His fate, but had remained close to Him each moment, suffering with Him as only a mother could. But even she could not save Him.

Jesus turned His gaze upon His grief-stricken mother and said to her, "Dear woman, here is your son." Then, addressing His disciple John, He said, "Here is your mother." (See John 19:26–27.) Even in the depths of His agony He continued to show His compassion.

John moved to stand by Mary who leaned against him as she looked on her Son in His last trial.

Then one of the criminals who were crucified with Jesus turned on Him, saying, "If you are the Christ, save yourself and us as well." (See Luke 23:39.)

Jesus did not answer, but looked at him with pity. The other criminal rebuked his companion, saying hoarsely, "We are receiving just punishment, but this man has done nothing wrong."

Then he turned, and in sincere tones said to Jesus, "These people who put you here are rejoicing because they think they have defeated you. But I can feel there is something about you which is far greater than any man. I don't understand it, but somehow I know that the essence of life exists in you. You are eternal." He paused in his agony. "O Lord! Will you remember me when you come into your kingdom?"

The Lord looked on him in his own anguish, and love from His spirit overshadowed and filled the man.

"Because you have asked from your heart, your prayer is answered. Truly I say to you, today you will be with me in paradise." (See Luke 23:40–43.)

This reply was like life given to the dead. Even though he was in the agonies of death, forgiveness and freedom flooded the heart of the criminal and he wept. He had been given a reprieve, but not from any earthly death sentence. He had been given heaven's pardon, a release from the powers of sin and death. He lost his fears. In his last moments all heaven had been secured for him through Jesus. His physical sufferings seemed to ease his body to rest, while his soul shone in the darkness and hovered over the death-gulf, ready to exit from death to life, from mortality to eternity.

The significance of this incident was missed by the mockers around the cross, but the angels and infants watched every detail in wonder and gratitude as Jesus revealed His divinity in this forgiveness. The impression made was so deep that from then on, whenever the children talked about the crucifixion, they would mention the thief's name and his prayer, together with the Redeemer's response, by which all of heaven was given to the dying sinner.

Death Defeated

D EEPER DARKNESS NOW began to shroud the scene. No sun or moon or stars were visible. Night veiled the earth.

After a long time, Jesus said, "I am thirsty" (John 19:28). Somebody filled a sponge with vinegar, put it on a stick and touched His parched lips. This sight was too much for the children so their guardians took them in their arms to support them.

A being of ghostly terror approached Jesus. Around him, circling like satellites, were multitudes of lesser creatures with the same appearance. A banner above him proclaimed: *you will triumph, you are king.*

He moved forward arrogantly, certain of victory in this mighty final conflict, a conflict which would settle the interests of the ages to come.

He spoke with a hoarse, sepulchral voice, a voice of terror, and addressed Jesus who still hung on the cross. "I rise up to greet you in this your day of madness. You are chained. You are victim. Angels, saints, and men have proclaimed your triumph over death, but let me tell you that my name is Death! You have set out to reverse the law by which I exist, the law that feeds the hungry graves. That law has always operated powerfully and no one can hinder it. This day it will grapple with you and you too will die. Look, I am about to smash you to pieces."

Then, reaching out his hand, he seized the body of Jesus, who quivered as the cold fingers closed around Him.

Jesus cried out, "Eloi, Eloi, lama sabachthani?...My God, my God, why have you forsaken me?" (Mark 15:34).

At His cry the voice of Justice rang out adamantly from above, "He must tread the winepress alone!" (See Isaiah 63:3.)

"He is doing this alone!" It was the voice of Mercy. "He is alone and He is suffering through it. He is dying for the world, the just for the unjust!"

Death shouted back: "Then I have won the victory! Jesus! He who was with God in the beginning! He has entered the place of death! He has gone there to rescue, but He has failed!

"Let Hades rise and see my triumph. You angelic hosts, look at Jesus struggling in my right hand! You have sung throughout heaven that He would conquer death! Now look at Him as I hold Him with my might. Single-handed I grasp this God-Man, and leap with Him among the tombs. Aha! Do you sing His victory? Sing His defeat instead! I hold the conqueror! Move back you heavens, before I come up and shake the eternal throne and make the heavenly worlds a cemetery for the dead."

With a wild exultant glare, he met the Savior's face. "How useless it was for you to attempt this. Haven't I slain unnumbered tens of thousands? Do you think that you can escape? No, Jesus, you God-Man, I sacrifice you, my last enemy."

Behind this I saw the triumphant Apollyon again. He was leading the hosts of evil spirits who were waving black banners. Emblazoned on the banners were two figures: Apollyon—the embodiment of evil, and Death—the ruthless destroyer. They were depicted embracing each other above the image of the cross and the bleeding sacrifice.

There was raucous shouting, blasphemies, and wild demoniacal laughter. The evil sounds washed back and forth like waves of thick black waters and their fiendish delight burst out like a blast from a compressed sea of madness. As Death stood there boasting, the evil spirits milled around him shouting in triumph, "Ah-ha! Ah-ha!"

The children watching this asked their guardians, "Will they win? Will Jesus die?"

An angel answered, "If Jesus dies, the heavens will end. He holds the universe in His right hand."

From a distance, Apollyon interrupted, "But in this decisive hour He has failed! Start singing your funeral dirge all of you, for look! 'Jesus! The Son of God' they boast! Now at last He has been subdued. Death is victorious!"

But Jesus, with every eye fixed on Him, rejoined, "No man can take my life from me. I have chosen to lay it down of my own free will. You, Death, have used men as your agents of slaughter and execution, but they have no power over me except what the Father has allowed them.[1] Look out! I am ready to burst through the portals of death to bind you, you destroyer, and rescue my people from your power. It is not revenge that I seek. I am coming to open the tomb and set the captives free."

Shaking himself free from Death's grasp He rose up to stand face to face with His ancient foe.

"I came down from heaven as a man. Because of this I have gained access to your dominion. Now I can destroy your power! You are conquered! The law of life will bind you and set boundaries to your rule. And I tell you, that day will come when death and hell will be thrown into the bottomless pit, and never again will they afflict my people."

Having said this He took hold of Death and tied him up with a chain of light.

Then, looking up to Justice who had watched all this from the cloud, He said, "Look! The Spirit of Life has defeated Death!"

Turning to the roaring tempest of disintegrating nature that was breaking up into storms around Him, He said, "You raging forces of death! Stop! Release your grip, you prince of terrors! I have come to rescue the fallen world before it plunges into the bottomless abyss."

As He stood in the mighty cataract of collapsing nature, He lifted His right hand to grasp the world, which had been drawn close to the abyss. It hovered over the brink, together with its swarming and lost millions of inhabitants, ready to plunge over the edge and into the surging billows that drove madly down into the gulf of death.

But He held it fast against every raging force, shouting to the tempest, "Stop, you great storm! Stop! In time past you have had invincible power to bring fear to the world, but now I command you to be still! Earth, return to your allotted domain. The day of your salvation has dawned."

He called to the heavens, "You mighty winds, fan this dying world into life. You waters of the eternal fountains of life, pour over her barren soil. You angels gather quickly and bring inspiration and truth to counteract perversion and lies.

"And you, Death," He roared, "though you boast of your millions slain, I set my seal on you. You are bound and your days are numbered. Hades, your kingdom of death—your trophy of the ages—will fail and at the appointed time you will die."

He spun around and faced Apollyon. "You enemy of justice! You enemy of peace and heaven! Go back to where you came from. Lead your forces to death, for at the appointed time you too will feel my restraining power. Look! I am coming to rescue my people."

Jesus finished these words with a great sweep of His hand, at which Apollyon and his legions fled. The dark cloud that followed hid them from our sight.

The Cross stood stark against the sky. Hanging in the extremity of His final agony, Jesus said, "Father, into your hands I commit my spirit," and with a loud voice He cried, "It is finished!" (John 19:30). Then, holding Death in His power,

107

He descended to the spirits in prison." (See 1 Peter 3:19.)

For a long time stillness filled the air. Nothing moved. No one spoke.

Gradually a soft light began to shine, revealing a solitary tomb guarded by armed men. An angel stood nearby. He touched the tomb with a scepter held in his right hand, and as he did so the tomb became transparent, revealing the body of Jesus.

It lay in the lone tomb, shrouded in clean linen, unstained by blood. The still and silent atmosphere, undisturbed by the clamor of the shouting rabble, brought soothing relief to the minds of the watching children. They had been overwhelmed by the scenes of cruelty and slaughter revealed during the sufferings of Jesus.

As we watched and enjoyed the quiet, the chief guardian spoke, "See how calm and composed the body of Jesus is now."

"Yes, Jesus is resting," answered a voice. Mercy appeared above the tomb. "He is resting. He is sleeping in the grave with His people. He has made the grave a holy place. But He will wake again. Not only that—He will also awaken all those who sleep in death."

Then one of the heavenly choirs descended over the tomb where Jesus lay and began to sing:

> Peace and holy rest,
> Hold the body of the Lord gently in your arms.
> It will never again endure pain.
> Holy angels, guard the sacred tomb.
> Do not let any intruder enter here
> Where the body of the Redeemer is resting.
> Hold back the forces of decay so that they do not
> harm it.
> It has been made holy through suffering.

Then, in loud acclamation, another company of angels sang:

> He will rise again. He will ascend to the highest
>   heaven.
> He will be the centerpiece and saints will gather
>   around.
> In the realms of immortality He will draw to Himself
> The renewed bodies of the saints.

Again the first choir sang:

> Let the heavens take up their lyres again
> And begin to sound their finest notes in lofty anthems.
> Jesus will awake and will ascend in clouds of glory.
> Universes will join the song of His ascension.
> Echo His name, you everlasting hills,
> Echo His name in triumphant song.

To see the body of Jesus rest in such sacred quietness filled me with a joy that was beyond description. To listen to the anthems of the angels watching the tomb was bliss.

It was true. Jesus had made the grave a holy place.

I can never reflect on that scene without feeling that my body should rest there also. I want to lay it down in the tomb. The grave is no longer gloomy for me. Rather, it is the most sacred place on earth. There, Jesus my Redeemer slumbered, His body free from pain. Just let me be worthy, and at the appointed time I will cheerfully lay my body to rest and await the morning of resurrection.

Twenty-Three

He Is Risen!

A MIGHTY ANGEL BROKE the stillness. Descending from above he stood on the tomb and shouted. "Look! The Son of man is coming from the place of death. Look! The Conqueror is coming!"

The spirit of Jesus appeared, walking among the tombs and looking over each one. "Sleeping bodies of my people, yours has been a long and dreary night, and your bed has been cold. You are the precious dust of the spirits I redeem. But you will rise and the darkness that has shrouded this place will be scattered by the light of life."

He strode on quickly. "I have come to light up this vault and set the limits of death and the grave. I have come to open a door of escape."

He paused. "Sleep on, you sacred dust of my people. Sleep on, until life from on high redeems and spiritualizes these remains. Then you will enter immortal and incorruptible spiritual life. Sleep on till that day, when you are called out of this slumber and into life. From now on the darkness of the tomb will be no more."

Looking up He said, "Watchman from the everlasting hills, come down and enter this place. Keep guard till the Resurrection morning when I will command you to rise with these ashes. Then they will be brought back to life and transformed into new bodies for my redeemed people. That day is coming with divine certainty."

In response, the watchman emerged from the mountain of light. He was mighty in strength, and light reflected from the ten thousand crosses woven into his garments. He bowed before Jesus. "I have come to do your will, O God."

The Lord replied, "Guard this grave where mortality is sleeping." He placed a scepter in the watchman's right hand. Engraved on its burnished shaft was the image of the cross and, in hieroglyphics, the solemn events of the trial and crucifixion. Jesus said, "Use this scepter to defend and control these dominions until heaven calls for you."

The watchman replied, "Be my helper! Your will be done forever!"

Our attention was then drawn to the lone tomb where the body of Jesus still lay, guarded by the angels. As we looked we saw the Holy Spirit approaching. With a voice of supreme power He cried out, "Let life descend! Let the life-giving Spirit fill this body! Let every part of it be transformed into life! Let this body be immortalized! Let it rise up!"

Light from the Holy Spirit surrounded the body and the walls and foundations of the tombs began to shake. Mighty tremors shook the earth again and again. And then the body of Jesus rose—He was alive!

A mighty angel cried out in a loud voice, "Jesus has conquered! He is rising up triumphant! Death has no power over Him! He has broken its chains! He is alive forever! Jesus reigns!"

"Hallelujah! Amen! Jesus reigns!" The overwhelming response erupted from countless watching angels.

Justice, still observing the scene, then spoke. "You shout about His victory, but He is still with the dead. He has not left there."

But Jesus was already advancing toward the massive gate that shut the way out from the tomb. Reaching out His hand He touched its heavy bars. "Open up, you mighty gate! Death, your keeper, has no more power over you. His limits have been determined." Instantly the bars crumbled to dust.

Looking over the ruins He said, "It is true that man has failed and broken the law of life. And it is true that his body will perish just as Adam's body perished. But now he will be restored by the law of life that I have revealed to mankind. He will live again! The grave shall not be ruler over the ashes of the dead. Neither will it exist forever as a valley of darkness between earth and heaven."

Jesus cried out again, "Open, you massive gate! And you winds carry it away so that it will never return!"

Immediately it was swept out of sight. Jesus then waved His right hand over the silent sleepers, saying, "This dust shall awake. It will be brought to life and it will be the dwelling place of the spirits of man." Then He rose from the tomb holding in His hand the keys of the dark dominions.

A voice spoke from the cloud that hovered above the scene, saying, "This is my beloved Son. Peace be to the world."

The cloud descended, and as it came close to Jesus, Mercy appeared from it and addressed Justice. "This is the offering I bring and this is the trophy of His victory—the once dead body of Jesus, now raised from the tomb and made immortal. Justice, do you accept this Offering?"

Justice replied, "The body has now been made immortal. Because of this I accept the Offering."

Mercy then said in satisfaction, "The Offering is now perfect. It is full of divine life and it will now be glorified. God himself, in the form of Jesus, came to save sinful man just as a faithful shepherd seeks out sheep that have strayed. From now on salvation will be preached to the lost, and those who receive it will find paradise.

"Jesus has mastered the fury of His enemies. Death will now give up its dead on the last day, when God will embrace all those who love and obey Him." (See 1 Thessalonians 4:16–17.)

Then Justice addressed Jesus. "You are from everlasting to

everlasting. You are King of kings and Lord of lords. You have the keys of death. heaven accepts your offering and acknowledges your victory. Your mission, trial and conquest are now inscribed on the throne of eternal remembrance. You are the Lamb slain for sinners. You are God."

Justice then embraced Jesus.

Mercy turned to Justice and asked, "The fallen sinner—can he be rescued now and receive God's favor?"

Justice replied, "God, in Christ, has intervened to reconcile mankind to Himself. Because of this, everyone who comes to God through Christ will be declared innocent. If people will stop pursuing what is evil and turn to the Lord, they will receive everlasting righteousness and peace in Jesus." (See Isaiah 55:7.)

With a radiant face Mercy looked up to heaven and said, "Salvation is complete. From now on your glory, O God, will shine on the fallen world. Your name will be adored by everyone who receives immortality."

On saying this, Mercy embraced Jesus. Then a cloud of light descended and encompassed Justice and Mercy. Their separate identities were fused together and from that time they were only ever seen as one—in the person of Jesus.

Then, surrounded by the cloud and the hallelujahs of thousands of thousands, this Jesus rose up from the tomb.

*   *   *   *   *

The scene moved on. The disciples had gathered on a mountaintop in obedience to the Lord's instruction and were discussing the Resurrection. Suddenly a light shone on them and Jesus appeared in their midst.

He said, "Do not be afraid. All authority in heaven and on earth has been given to me. Therefore go and preach the good news to all nations, baptizing them in the name of the Father and of the Son and of the Holy Spirit. Teach them to obey everything I have commanded you. And surely I will always be with you, to the very end of the age." (See Matthew 28:18–20.)

"People will persecute you for my name's sake, but because I have overcome you will also overcome, if you trust my Word.[1]

"And these signs will accompany those who believe: In my name they will drive out demons; they will speak in new tongues; they will pick up snakes with their hands; and when they drink deadly poison, it will not hurt them at all; they will place their hands on sick people, and they will get well (Mark 16:17–18). But wait in the city of Jerusalem until you have received power from on high." [2]

Then He lifted up His hands and blessed them. As He was blessing them He was taken up and a cloud hid Him from their sight. (See Acts 1:9.)

Then the unnumbered millions who filled the heavens, took up their instruments and with powerful voices sang, "We give you thanks, O Lord God Almighty, who was and is and is to come, because You have taken Your great power and conquered.[3] We praise you, O Lord. You are King of kings, Lord of lords, the Alpha and Omega, the Beginning and the End; the First and the Last."[4]

The disciples continued to look toward heaven where their risen and ascended Lord had gone but eventually the cloud which hid Him from their sight disappeared. Then they worshipped. After that they rose up silently and departed for Jerusalem.

The Lost Man Rescued

ITH THE CLOSING of these scenes, an angel appeared and proclaimed with a loud voice, "Salvation has come! Take heart and rejoice you inhabitants of the earth! The Lion of the tribe of Judah, the Root of David, has triumphed. He is able to open the scroll and its seven seals (Rev. 5:5). Let salvation, the year of jubilee, be preached to the far places.[1] Go out, you messengers! Declare this love of God to the lost human race. Yes! Let the heavens echo the good news. For God so loved the world that he gave his one and only Son, that whoever believes in him shall not perish but have eternal life" (John 3:16).

But even as the angel spoke we heard a mournful voice crying out, "Help me! I am in terrible trouble! Who will rescue me from this wretched dying body?" (See Romans 7:24.)

From the direction of the voice a cloud rose up in the middle of a terrible storm. A little beyond that cloud I could see high mountains with terrifying fire and smoke pouring from their sides.

Again I heard the voice crying in anguish, "Do we have to die?"

The dark cloud which hung over the scene then parted and a pale light revealed the dying man and his family once again. Beside them now was a man, simply dressed, holding a book in his hand. He read from it, "Come to me, all

115

you who are weary and burdened, and I will give you rest" (Matt. 11:28).

As he read, the suffering man looked up. He seemed startled by the presence of the stranger, but asked him, "Who will give me rest? Who are you talking about?"

He replied, "Jesus, who is the Savior of men, will help you."

"But I am unclean, every part of me."

The messenger read again from the book: "Though your sins are like scarlet, they shall be as white as snow; though they are red as crimson, they shall be like wool" (Isa. 1:18).

The man groaned, "But I have sinned against heaven."

Again the messenger read, "Let the wicked forsake his way, and the evil man his thoughts. Let him turn to the LORD, and he will have mercy on him, and to our God, for he will freely pardon" (Isa. 55:7). Then he added, "It is also written, 'It is not the healthy who need a doctor, but the sick' (Matt. 9:12). If you want to enter into life with all your heart you may do so. Look up!" he continued, as he raised his hand.

Immediately a light shone from above and the man saw the Redeemer on the cross. At the same time he heard a voice saying, "He who believes in me will live, even though he dies; and whoever lives and believes in me will never die. Do you believe this?...I am the way and the truth and the life. No one comes to the Father except through me" (John 11:25–26; 14:6).

The suffering man replied, "Lord, I do believe, but help me overcome my doubts" (Mark 9:24). Lifting his hands he prayed, "God, have mercy on me, a sinner" (Luke 18:13).

With this, a light descended and touched him and the Spirit of God filled his soul.

"Your sins have been forgiven, your guilt is removed, your wounds have been healed. The Spirit has made you alive and is now telling you to get up, for you have received salvation."

The redeemed man stood up. His face was transfigured and he began to worship. The light that shone on him revealed the image of the cross inscribed on his inner being and the law of heaven written on his heart.

The messenger, still at his side, now read, "Blessed are the pure in heart, for they will see God" (Matt. 5:8). Then he said, "You have been brought to life by the Spirit. You have passed from death to eternal life.[2] You are now wearing the clothes of salvation.[3] The Spirit is telling you to go out and tell the many who need to hear all about the grace of God.[4] Go and preach the good news. Seek out the lost. You have received freely, now give freely.[5]

"Be faithful to what has been given to you. Be on guard, so that when your Lord comes and calls you, you can give a good account of your work for him." (See Matthew 25:14–46.)

He read again, "Look! God is with you to bless you and strengthen you. His grace will enable you to face every trial you may have." (See 2 Corinthians 12:9.)

The redeemed man looked up and prayed, "Help me God. I can do anything if Jesus Christ strengthens me." (See Philippians 4:13.)

Then, transformed into a servant of the cross and an ambassador of Jesus, he entered the cloud that had darkened the plain at the foot of the mountain. As he departed we heard his voice.

"Lord, I really am Your servant. You took off all my chains. What can I give You for all You have done for me? I will always praise You and thank You.[6] Search me, then, O God, by your Spirit, and test me. See if there is any wrong way in me and always lead me in your ways."[7]

His final words were filled with joy. "Praise the Lord all you nations, for His mercy and kindness to us is tremendous. Praise the Lord!"

Then a vast company of redeemed spirits, led by Jesus' mother Mary, joined in and sang: "We will praise You, O Lord God Almighty, who was and is, and is to come, for the wonderful things You have done for all people! Your ways are just and true! You have redeemed us! Even when we were not even thinking about You, Your Spirit sought us out! Worthy is the Lamb! Your works are wonderful! You live above the cherubim, Your throne is eternal, Your dominion is over all! Praise, glory, and sovereignty to You throughout everlasting ages! Amen!"

Finally, an angel said to me, "The children are now ready to ascend to a higher plane. They will learn even greater things and will rise further and further from there. The glory of that place is now descending and the spirits who will take these little ones up there are now receiving them from their former guardians. Let us go."

Twenty-Five

Return to Earth

THE TIME AT last drew near when I was to return to the world. The children, their attending angels and those who had watched the various scenes, gathered around me and sang a hymn. More than ever I felt their love and the marvelous worth of heaven.

The spirit who had earlier kissed the cross approached me, leading the two children as before, and said, "Marietta, you have to leave us now. We love you and deeply sympathize with you that you have to depart. But it is our Redeemer's command, so we will cheerfully submit to that. But Marietta, we rejoice because we know you will return at the appointed time."

"Yes, we are looking forward to that," responded one in the crowd. "We are so happy that you were able to see some of the beautiful things—the heavenly homes and the angelic worship. But even more than that, we really praise our heavenly Father for showing you how children are taught about man's sinful nature and how He has provided for his redemption.

"It is just wonderful to know that you have been received by the Redeemer Himself and blessed by Him. We give you all our love and will wait very patiently till we greet you at the gate of the Holy City when you return. That will be a happy time!"

Then they all stood in a circle around me. The spirit who

had first addressed me, hugged me and I felt all of their love in that single embrace. Thinking about that scene now, it fills me with indescribable peace and delight.

After this, the spirit led the two children to me. They wrapped their arms around my neck and kissed me many times, saying, "Marietta, when you return to the world and meet again with those who loved us and mourned our loss—tell them we are happy here. Tell them we have no sorrow. We are always with our guardians and we love everyone—and Jesus our Redeemer above all. Tell them we are waiting patiently for their arrival here. We love you too, Marietta, and will meet you again."

Then Jesus descended from a cloud. Placing His hand on my head he spoke to me.

"Child, it is important that you return. You have a commission. Be faithful to it. Whenever you have an opportunity, tell people what you have seen and heard. Fulfill your mission and, at the appointed time, angels will meet you at the gate of death and carry you to your home here in the kingdom of peace. Do not be sad. My grace will uphold you. In your sufferings you will be supported."

Then an angel gave Him a golden goblet and He placed it to my lips. As I drank I was filled with new life and courage so that I could endure the separation. I bowed and worshipped Him.

Then with His right hand He raised me up, saying, "Child of sorrow from a world of gloom, you are redeemed, you are blessed forever. Be faithful, and when your time on earth is ended, you will enter into the joy of your Lord."

Then, placing an olive branch in my hand, He said, "Take this to earth, as you have been instructed." Once again He laid His hand on my head and light and love filled my spirit.

The time had come for my departure. I looked around on that lovely city and its happy inhabitants. In thanksgiving I offered myself to God for the blessings of immortality and, above all, for the gift of grace in Jesus, the Redeemer. In front of all the crowds, I lifted my hands to the Lord and prayed for support, that I might be kept in the love of Jesus who had blessed me. Then I was carried in the arms of angels to the gateway of the temple where I first met the Lord.

From that point, as angels sang praise to God and the Lamb, my guide and I descended to earth. On entering this room where my body lay, I soon woke up.

Now I am waiting patiently for that time which has been predetermined, when I will go and forever enjoy those happy places where I found assurance of the joys to come. I praise God for my hope in Jesus. It is worth ten thousand worlds to me.

When I arrive in paradise, free from mortality, I will praise Him with a pure and undivided heart. I will exalt the name of my Redeemer in loud anthems throughout eternity.

Original Testimonies

T HE FOLLOWING TESTIMONIALS are presented here in their original form, except for a few slight changes where words have altered significantly in meaning or were particularly difficult to understand. Although obviously different in style to our language of today they are quite easy to follow— unlike the language of the main text of the original book.

Statement of Original Publisher

The increasing demand for this work, with so little effort to call public attention to it, confirms our first impressions, that it is the Book for the age; one greatly needed to supply the deficiency intuitively sensed by the mind of the present generation.

Edition after edition has been published and passed silently into the hands of the reading public. Reports of an encouraging nature reach us from all sections where it has found its way; and the united testimony of those who avail themselves of the work is, that, to read is to be benefited.

Its sound theology, purely religious sentiment, and thrilling descriptions of scenes enacted beyond the grave, as seen by the spirit of the young girl, while her body lay entranced, cannot, it seems to me, fail to strengthen the faith of the Christian in the truths of Revelation. More particularly is it adapted to the youthful mind of this age, to awaken in it a love of the Christian Religion as it unfolds so graphically the great plan of man's Redemption—"which things the angels desire to look into."

I have witnessed its effect upon the youthful mind. They, while listening to the thrilling story of Marietta, seem borne along with her enraptured spirit, and with it to witness the unfolding of visions, by which the Infants are being taught to know their Redeemer, that they too, might be able to realize and love Him, who was once a babe in a manger; then a man of sorrows acquainted with grief; then suffering death and triumphing over the grave, for the redemption of a ruined and forlorn race.

I unhesitatingly state it as my firm and unwavering belief, that the spirit of Marietta Davis, like John, the Revelator, while his body was in the Isle of Patmos, visited scenes beyond the grave, and there saw and heard what she relates. However this may be, if the truth can be brought to reach the mind, and win the affections to the Christian Religion, all is gained that should be desired.

—STEPHEN DEUEL
DAYTON, OHIO
SEPTEMBER 1, 1856

Testimonies Authenticating the Vision

The following testimonials from the mother and sisters of Marietta Davis; and from Emerson Hull, M.D., who has been a resident of Berlin for many years, and is a physician of eminence, are but a part of those in possession of the editor, but are considered sufficient to authenticate the narrative.

1. Testimony of the family, Berlin, NY, Nov. 15, 1855
Rev. J. L. Scott:
Dear Friend,
        Since you have been publishing the trance of Marietta Davis, in the Mountain Cove Journal, some of the

readers have written to us to ascertain its authenticity. Upon this account, and to relieve you from embarrassment, we submit the following for your disposal: Marietta Davis was a member of our family; she was born in this town, where she lived until called by death from us.

She was not of open religious habits; being disinclined to religious conversation. During the revival in the winter of 1847–1848, her mind, as you well know, was religiously exercised; but she could not obtain the reality of the faith others had found, so as to enable her to join her young friends in the truths of the Gospel. In August following she fell into a sleep, or trance, from which she could not be awakened. In that state she remained nine days; and when she awoke, she said she had been in heaven; that she had seen there many of her old friends and relations who were dead; and Jesus the Redeemer. From that time her hope in heaven, through Jesus, was strong; and she rejoiced in the prospect of a final admission into the Paradise of Peace.

During her short stay with us, after she came out of the trance, she related what she said she had seen, heard, and learned during her sleep; but much of what she told us, she said she wished should not be mentioned then, for the world was not prepared to hear it. The trance, as you published it, as far as we can recollect, is correct; only you have omitted much. Marietta fell asleep in August, 1848, and died the following March, and at the time and in the manner predicted by herself.

Yours,

Nancy Davis, Mother
Susan Davis, Sister
Sarah Ann Davis, Sister

2. Testimony of the attending physician, Berlin, NY, Nov. 15, 1853

Rev. J. L. Scott:
Dear Sir,

In the Summer of 1848, with yourself, I visited the widow Nancy Davis, of this town, in the capacity of medical attendant upon her daughter Marietta, who had fallen into a state of catalepsy, or trance, in which she remained nine days, and from which to awaken her human skill seemed unavailing. When she returned to her normal state, she related much of a remarkable character, which she said she had learned while in the trance.

Having read portions of what you have published in the Mountain Cove Journal, I am prepared to give my testimony as to its strict correspondence to what I heard her relate before her death.
Your Obedient Servant,
Emerson Hull, MD

3. Testimonies of prominent ministers living at the time of the vision

Lest some who have not read this Trance, and are therefore unacquainted with its character, should class it with books "got up" by the "spirit media" of the day, and to assure the reader that its correct sentiment and pure spirit commend it to the confidence of the Religious Public, we insert the following statements of the Rev. Mr. Waller, of Kentucky, and the Rev. Mr. Miller, of Springfield, Ohio.

Rev. G. Walker, one of the first ministers of the Baptist order, in Kentucky, whose sound Theology and good sense won him, for twenty-five consecutive years, the highest office in his denomination, and whose name is sufficient commendation for any Work through the wide field of his usefulness, and wherever his name is known, writes as follows:

"I have carefully examined a book bearing the title: 'Scenes Beyond the Grave,' purporting to be a simple

narrative of scenes enacted beyond the grave, and
witnessed by the spirit of a young girl while she lay
entranced, as the testimony shows. Of this I express
no opinion; but fully approve of its pure and deep-tone
spirit of Christianity, and sound Theology.

"The Scenes are so truly depicted, and so beautifully
and thrillingly told, that it cannot fail to secure the
judgment, and win the confidence and affections of all
who read it.

"I am constrained to say, that in purity of style, and
richness of composition, it is not excelled by any work
I have read. I should be pleased if it could be placed
upon the table of every family, and read in every
common and Sunday school in the land. Disbelief in
Christianity can have little influence where it is read.
It is particularly adapted to the use of families and
schools, to form in the young mind the first impressions. I therefore, very cheerfully recommend it to the
public, and particularly to all who love the Bible and
the Christian religion."
George Waller
Louisville, Kentucky
June 15, 1855

* * * * *

Rev. Mr. Miller, of Springfield, Ohio, Minister of the Meth-
odist Episcopal Church, a man of deep devotion and marked
piety who has not only the confidence of his Church, but for
some twenty years has held a responsible office—the gift of
the people of his city and county—in a letter speaks thus:
Rev. J. L. Scott:

"I have before me the first part of the Trance of Marietta
Davis, entitled 'Scenes Beyond the Grave,' which I have read
with inexpressible delight; and it so far exceeds any work I
have previously read, which treats upon the lost state of man,

and his redemption through our Lord Jesus Christ, that I am constrained to urge upon you the necessity of placing it in the hands of every family in the land.

"Its richness, and purity of style, its poetic grandeur and figurative excellence, so possess the mind of the reader, that he seems himself 'entranced,' and borne far beyond the darkness and imperfections of earth, to be an observer with the spirit of Marietta, of the lovely scenes that occupy the inhabitants of heaven; and also as was revealed to her, the reader realizes most deeply the depth of iniquity into which man is fallen by reason of sin, and becomes lost in the contemplation of the boundless goodness bestowed in his redemption.

"Her description, as revealed to her, of the display of Justice, and Mercy, the meekness, love and suffering of the Saviour, in the purpose and completion of the plan of Salvation, is unequalled; and the narrative of what she saw in Paradise, where the infants from earth are received, agreeing so perfectly as it does with our highest hopes of the blessedness of our little ones, who have departed this life, fills the reader with ecstasy.

"No language of mine is in any way capable of explaining the feelings that awaken in the soul, while reading the narrative, and whatever may have been the inspiring cause (and I believe she saw what she relates), I feel that whoever reads the Trance with any degree of care will receive from it, lasting benefit.

"I am therefore eager that it should be spread abroad through the land, and the more especially, since it is so well calculated to counteract the destructive influence of the disbelief in Christianity, now so abundantly proclaimed by the advocates of modern Infidel Spiritualism.

In the bonds of Christian affection, I am yours,
Reuben Miller
Springfield, Clark Co., Ohio
June 9, 1855

4. Testimony of Marietta's pastor

The work now presented to the public as depicting *Scenes Beyond the Grave*, does not come without authority for its somewhat startling title. In the summer of 1848, a young woman named Marietta Davis, aged twenty-five years, residing with her mother Mrs. Nancy Davis, at Berlin, New York, fell into a sleep or trance, in which she remained for nine days. All endeavours on the part of her friends and of her physicians failed to arouse her from this unnatural state. When at last she awoke to a consciousness of external things, she was in the full possession of all her natural faculties, with an almost supernatural acuteness of perception superadded. Before she fell into the trance, her mind had been considerably exercised in regard to her future state; but there was yet a lingering doubt which greatly disturbed her. Her mother and sisters were exemplary members of a Baptist Church, in Berlin, then under my pastoral charge, but Marietta's doubt seemed to have kept her from the enjoyment of the hope in which her family so confidently rested. But when she came out of the trance, in which she had lain for so many days, it was with joy and rejoicing over the unspeakable things which she had seen and heard. Her mouth was filled with praises to God, and her heart swelled with gratitude to him for his loving kindness. She averred that while her body lay as it were in death, her spirit had visited the eternal world. She informed her friends that she was not to remain long with them: but should soon go hence to enjoy a mansion prepared for her in her heavenly Father's Kingdom. After this she lived seven months and died at the time predicted by herself; and so perfectly did she know the hour of her departure, that when it arrived she selected a hymn and commenced singing it with the family; and while they sang, her spirit took its flight so gently as not to attract attention. Thus the hymn commenced with her friends on earth, and doubtless concluded with the angels in heaven.

The style of Marietta's narrative is peculiar. She regretted her inability to express her conceptions of what she had seen and heard, so as to give a definite idea of the glories of the heavenly world. I have not felt at liberty to change the style of her narrative, and as far as possible have employed her own language. Having received the story from her own lips, I have so preserved it, as to make it in truth the relation of her own experience.

The tone of the trance is exalted and Christlike; and therefore its influence cannot fail to be of a useful and sacred character. Confident of this, I offer it to the public. If read in the spirit in which it was given, it cannot fail to gladden and encourage the Christian, and to lead the thoughts of the man of the world beyond his material existence. For while following her in her wide range of spiritual thoughts and visions, forgetting the outer world, we fancy that the heavens are opened to our view, revealing their glory and magnificence. We seem to see the moving multitudes, who with golden harps and angelic voices are chanting praises to God. With ecstasy we behold, as mirrored before us, the Infant Paradise; and appear ourselves to be observing the order and harmony of the inhabitants of that divine sphere. Then borne onward and upward by her entrancing story, in the spirit we seem to arise with saints and angels and become familiar with the inhabitants of the Celestial heavens, and are led to exclaim, "Marietta! You favoured of heaven, we bless that Providence which unfolded your vision, while we read with delight of soul, the revelations of your entranced spirit!"

J. L. Scott

Infant Paradise

*T*HE FOLLOWING FOUR *chapters were originally located in the story immediately after chapter five. They describe in detail the care of infants and children in a special nursery in paradise. The section is fairly self-contained and has been placed here in order to establish a consistent pace throughout the rest of the story. Continuing from the end of chapter five, the boy finishes his conversation with Marietta:*

"The passing angel who paused before us just now was the one who carried me to the place prepared for young and fragile children. These angel spirits are continually nourishing their little minds. Would you like to visit that nursery?"

He looked up at the spirit, as if to ask permission to take me there.

Infant Instructions and Care

In a moment we were moving upwards, in the direction taken by the angel with the baby. Before long we approached a city, built in the middle of a plain covered in flowers. I saw stately buildings and streets lined with shady trees. Birds of all colors perched in the branches, their different notes blending together in perfect harmony. Many were the same as birds I knew on earth, but they were far more beautiful—just as the paradise itself was so much more glorious than earth.

As we journeyed on, the beauty and harmony increased with each new panorama. I was struck by the stunning architecture of the buildings and magnificent sculptures outside them. Fountains sparkled in the light and beautiful trees waved their outstretched branches. The interwoven flowers and flowering vines became more beautiful the further I went. I also saw many avenues, winding up toward a common central point.

As we headed to this point a vast and complex structure rose in front of us. The outer walls and towers seemed to be made of marble, delicate as snow in appearance. This structure was the foundation for a vast canopy, like a dome, yet far bigger than any similar earthly dome could ever be. As we drew near I saw that the dome was suspended over a vast circular space.

"This dome," said my guide, "is the place where all infants from earth are gathered for instruction. The outer buildings are the nurseries where we bring them first of all, to be nourished by their guardian angel.

"Each nursery is a miniature of the vast instruction dome, but it is nevertheless unique. These are the homes for the infant spirits until they develop sufficiently to enter the paradise of youth where the instruction is more advanced. Each nursery has seven maternal guardians over it.

"You can see, Marietta that no two buildings are decorated alike, yet they all blend harmoniously together. Also, each guardian angel has a different appearance and a different radiant light.

"Whenever an infant dies on earth, the guardian angel who brings it here assesses all of its abilities and places it with others of similar ability. According to its artistic, scientific, or social abilities, each is given a home best suited to the development of those gifts.

"Each building is directed by a group of seven maternal guardian angels. Each one has a similar type of mind to the others, and works perfectly with them.

"Each day, or at special times, the infants are taken out to the center dome for their teaching and development.

"When they have progressed, they are moved from their homes and enter the general assembly in the great center dome of instruction. When this happens an angelic choir forms a cloud above them, singing alleluias to their Prince and Savior."

As the spirit finished speaking, to my amazement I saw on our right, the wall of one of the nurseries being removed, as though an invisible hand had drawn aside a curtain. I was able to see completely inside. Supremely bright, it was adorned with great artistic beauty, in keeping with the splendor of the entire paradise of infants.

At first I felt ashamed and unworthy to even look at a place so pure and lovely. Almost without realizing, I cried out, "This is heaven!"

My instructress responded, "Marietta, this is something of what infant life is like in paradise. We will go in and you can see even more. Mortals know so little of the happiness of their little ones who die as babies."

We walked along together.

"Those who believe in Christ become reconciled to their loss when they submit in their hearts. I was once a mother in the world of sorrow and loss. I learned what it was to farewell a baby who came into the world only to break my heart at death. I learned to weep but I also learned the priceless value of faith in God's mercy through our Lord Jesus Christ.

"Three times I held my beloved babies in my arms. They were flesh of my flesh, bone of my bone, and life of my life. I looked up to God and adored Him for the precious gifts. But I had hardly begun to love them and look forward to the future when they were gone, and I was left sad and wounded."

Her face showed the sorrow she had once felt.

"I trusted in Jesus, and gave them over to Him, believing they were well. But, Marietta, if I had only known, if I could have only seen what you see! Adding my faith to that knowledge would have given me a much greater peace. For the baby who left its parents in such sadness, waits here for their arrival safe from the evils of sin. Look, Marietta," her face brightened, "look at them."

As I looked, another section of the interior suddenly opened before me. It was a beautifully decorated temple. In circular tiers, one rising above another, I saw small niches shaped like segments of circles. In each lay an infant spirit attended by a guardian angel. Each angel's task was to prepare the infant for higher existence, to enable it to make a holy and fruitful contribution in its never-ending life. The angel breathed upon the baby and each breath caused its capacity and life to expand. It instilled holy love and inspiration, for its power came from God. God's life-giving Spirit permeates all angels in heaven.

As we entered the nursery I watched the infants as they awoke to a still greater consciousness. They looked back at their angels bending over them and gave them beautiful smiles.

If only I could properly describe even this one nursery! If only I could fix it in your mind so that you could fully appreciate its glorious magnificence! Then I would be happier! But I am not able to do so. How mere words frustrate me!

I saw other angels whose task it was to play music on a variety of instruments. The music mingled continually with angelic voices, all so soft and beautiful. It was life-giving, bringing energy and strength to the infants as they lay there beside their smiling guardians.

"This," said my guide, "is only one of many great temples or nurseries, all of them similar. If only earthly parents could realize it, this is like the birth place of those who leave their bodies before they reach understanding. From here they go up to places specially prepared for them. But Marietta, you have still not seen the most delightful part of this temple."

Jesus and the Infant

As she spoke, each of the guardian angels rose with their infant, and stood poised in the great area around the angel who held the cross. As they did, a brilliant light descended from above lighting up a majestic retinue of angels surrounding the glorious Redeemer. I was completely awed by the scene.

As they approached the center, the vision of the cross faded away in the dazzling light. The angel retinue paused and the Redeemer smiled and said, "Bring these little ones to me" (Matt. 19:14). I was overwhelmed by the sweetness and gentleness of this gesture and the love that shone from His face. My knees gave way and I sank at the feet of my heavenly guide, but she raised me up and embraced me.

I wish that the whole world could see and hear what happened next.

As the Redeemer spoke, the guardian angels came forward, and presented their charges to Him. He held His hand above them, and goodness, like dew-drops, literally fell from it. The infants seemed to drink from these drops as if they were a fountain of living water. Each drop brought them a liberating freedom that was the very breath of life. They responded in sheer delight at the wonderful experience.

Songs of redemption then rose from the attending angels as they played together on stringed instruments. The Redeemer waved His hand to thank them, and they bowed in response, and veiled their faces in the garment of glory that subsequently enveloped them.

Then the angels in each nursery responded with their own songs, and the music swelled and rolled around the vast temple as the Redeemer and His angels rose out of sight. With that, the angels of the temple went back to their tasks.

My guide spoke to me, "This is the simplest part of bringing up infant spirits here. It is such a happy task, seeing them develop. Earth would have been the proper place for it, but men and women left their original purity and broke their relationship with the exalted heavenly beings who could have helped this growth and maturing process." (See Genesis 3.)

"Marietta, it was sin that brought about the difference between mankind and angels. It completely changed man's moral nature. Angels are pure and untainted. They have no evil desires to stir up wrong in them and only the purest life flows from them.

"That life nourishes others. Dependent spirits can flourish because of the influence of exalted angels. Then, in the same way, these exalted angels flourish in the glory of even higher groups of angels. Following on, these higher groups benefit from the influence of a still higher class of beings. In that way, all pure spiritual beings are united and live in spheres of higher life. Then, as one great body, they live in the life which comes down from God, who is the Life of all.

"Unbelieving and rebellious people are cut off from these higher natures. They don't know what they have lost, nor do they realize their need of the Savior-Redeemer. He is the only one who can restore the lost relationship. In this place the mature come to understand the law of salvation and life in Christ, and so come to adore their Redeemer."

She took my arm. "You noticed after the Redeemer blessed the infants all the nurseries burst into praise. That was completely spontaneous. Those who know the effects of sin are well able to recognize the humility and mercy of Jesus, and they adore Him from their inmost being. When He moves amongst them they sing silently inside, but as He withdraws they sing out loud. Marietta, these happy beings could no more hold back their joy and thanksgiving than life could stop flowing from Jesus. It is like that throughout heaven, but especially in the places of preparation for the spirits of the redeemed." My guide whispered in awe. "Did you realize that each breath around you is actually a separate song of praise to God?"

She burst out again, "If only men on earth knew how good God is in providing redemption for them! They would stop doing wrong and learn righteousness and the ways of peace. Marietta, do you understand this?"

I felt the reproof, remembering my lack of faith in Jesus' salvation. I wished I could hide myself from the scrutiny of the spirit speaking to me. I had often questioned whether man lives forever and doubted that he could be restored from wrong-doing through the Lord Jesus Christ. But now I realized that Jesus is everything and in everything. He is the source of every pure and holy delight, and the center of everything I had been allowed to see in the world of spirits.

When the angels returned to tending the infants, my guide told me that the baby spirits were now to be passed on to another group of angels for the next stage of their advancement. In this process I would witness the reception of new infants from earth.

Above me and all around, I saw a new group of angels poised, waiting to enter the temple with the new infants. When the first angels had given up their previous charges the new angels entered and filled the central area around the cross.

"These angels are of a more exalted nature," said my guide. "They are encompassed in a light even greater than that of the temple, and they radiate a halo of light which gives life and love. See it is intensifying and enveloping the infant spirits.

"This light carries a soft music that touches every fiber of their being. As they hear it the Holy Spirit is transforming them and increasing their capacity. Each part of the infant is brought together perfectly, bringing health and energy and expansion to their system. This develops their intellect, their judgment and understanding, and allows them to enjoy life to the full."

Restoration of an Infant

We paused as a shaft of light moved over us. It enabled me to see that these delicate infants were actually incomplete and unable to function. Each part of them lay separately, able to move but without control, moving only in spasms. They reminded me of beautiful musical instruments, but without strings.

Puzzled by it all I questioned my guide. "When I first saw an infant spirit, it seemed so fragile I thought it would die. But a light shone down on it and it moved, as though it had received life and energy. But now I can see the tissues and organs of the infant and they are all broken apart. Can they ever be restored? They are so complex!"

For my answer I was once again surrounded by light. It revealed the many functions of the infant's spirit responding to the touch of an invisible power so that they blended and adapted to each other in perfect harmony. When they joined together they lost their separate identities and became a single being, full and perfect.

Unconsciously I uttered the words, "Praise God for His mighty works," for I was now looking at an infant restored; a spirit in all the perfection of angelic life. Looking up into the face of the angels it smiled. I reflected on my first sight of the child, scarred by the effects of the sin-cursed world, and then looked again at this brand new life. I remembered the Bible text, "Do not be surprised that I said to you, you must be born again." (See John 1:12–13; 3:1–17.) I felt also the force of David's words in the Psalms: "I am fearfully and wonderfully made" (Ps. 139:14). Turning to my guide I asked, "Is this real? Is this the redemption of a spirit?"

"Yes," said my guide, "What you have seen has really taken place. It is the work of grace on a spirit corrupted by sin."

She paused and choked on the words, "Sin, that violation of the law of God! Marietta! The quality that was lost in this infant because of sin could not be restored simply by things like light descending from angels or by their beautiful music. The guardian angels could not supply it either. They can only give support during the process.

"The only one who has the power to do this work of restoration is the Redeemer. He tunes each fiber of the infant's being, purifying and breathing the life of holiness into the soul to give new life, health, energy, will and love. He then brings this new being into a perfect life. So now you see a spirit made complete by redemption.

"Marietta, treasure this in your heart. Remember, too, that this is only one infant of the many you have seen in this nursery."

A wave of sound caught my attention. "Now listen, Marietta. Can you hear those angels? They are singing praises to God and the Lamb for redemption. There are multitudes of these spirits, and they always thank God like this when a newborn spirit is brought into heaven."

I looked up and my spirit caught fire as the song rose, wave after wave in ascending praise, adoration and glory—inexpressible and divine! As John said in the book of Revelation, it was like "the roar of rushing waters" (Rev. 1:15; 14:2; 19:6). It seemed that the whole city became one voice of praise.

"So this is heaven!" I exclaimed.

It must be wonderful to be considered worthy of entering the city of God! And if this is only the infant paradise, if this is only the song for the restoration of infant spirits, how much greater will the praise be when the redemption of all mankind is complete! How wonderful that day will be! All of the redeemed—the Bride of the Lamb—will take up golden harps to praise Him as they rise from the great marriage supper in heaven.

The happiness I experienced was so uplifting that I attempted to join in with the beautiful songs of praise. But as I did, memories of my unworthiness overcame me, and I fell into the arms of my guide.

Infants Worship at the Cross

Looking up into the face of my heavenly guardian I saw an expression of deep emotion sweep over her. Her eyes were fixed earnestly above and her lips moved as if in prayer. At first she looked so sad that I thought she would weep, but I could tell that tears would have been only a poor expression of such deep and profound feeling. I wondered to myself, *Is it possible that angels can grieve? Can sorrow enter this Holy City?*

The music stopped and its echo faded slowly in the distance. Silence reigned over the vast area. I did not dare to move. Then a light from above shone on my protector with increasing brilliance. Her eyes were still fixed, but her breathing became deeper, her lips still and her glowing face took on an expression of deepest reverence. I was so awed by her emotion that I did not notice the cause of it until, without turning her eyes, she gently touched my head and pointed.

With utter astonishment I took in the scene before us. There!! Oh! I wish all the world knew it! There, hanging on the cross, bleeding and dying—my Lord and Redeemer! Oh! That sight! No human heart can know how it affected the spirits who serve in the infants' paradise. The crown of thorns, the nails, the mangled form, the flowing blood, the look of compassion, all were so plainly revealed to me. They told of the most intense and excruciating suffering.

From every part of the city, guardian angels with their infant spirits were gathered around the cross in deep humility and holy reverence. The angels held out the infant spirits in their care, showing them the cross and the Sacrifice. Then an angel descended, clothed in bright garments. He moved around the cross, holding his glittering crown in his hand. Then, bowing, he worshipped in silence like all who had gathered there.

Turning to the guardian angels he said, "Adore Him, because He is the Redeemer of a fallen race. Let all heaven adore Him!" He lifted up his right hand and I saw in it a little book. Following suit, all the angels did the same, each holding a book of similar size.

At this point a choir of angels appeared. They had palms in their hands and with one voice they sang praise to God and to the Lamb. I could not understand the first song but they finished with the words that the Redeemer spoke long ago: "Let the children come to me. The kingdom of heaven belongs to such as these. God has ordained that little ones will bring him perfect praise." (See Luke 18:16; Matthew 21:16; Psalm 8:2.) Amen, alleluia, amen!

Then the guardian angels drew closer to the cross. Presenting the infants in their care they were addressed by the angel with the glittering crown, but the message was entirely beyond my understanding. Following this, each infant was touched with a stream of light. They smiled and bowed their heads, and held up in their tiny clasped hands the image of the cross which the angels had given them.

Once again they were cradled in the arms of their protectors, and the choir sang another anthem. The surrounding spirits joined in, filling the city with the sound. Then the cross and the Sacrifice disappeared and the angels returned to their places.

During all this my guide had not moved or spoken but seemed to be totally absorbed in what was taking place.

After a while I asked, "Can heaven exist without the cross and Sacrifice? I am learning that the cross is at the center of everything here. Every spirit reveres it, and each hymn of praise mentions the name of the Sacrifice."

She replied with solemn emphasis, "The cross is always in the minds of redeemed spirits. You see it in every aspect of this place. Every flower and every artistic work has the cross in it—as though an invisible hand has woven it throughout. It is the symbol of redeeming love, and all instruction given here is based on it.

"The guardian angels teach the infants about redemption through Jesus and His suffering on the cross. Each group is instructed so that the cross and the Sacrifice are firmly implanted on their minds. In this way the truth of the cross and Sacrifice becomes part of their lives.

"All redeemed spirits are treated in this way. When a soul is stamped with the cross, the resulting glow is obvious to every angel and redeemed person. Because of this, evil spirits or wicked beings cannot hide their real nature. Where the cross does not shine there is no pure love, and no peace with God. Marietta, in heaven there is no possibility of deceit.

"But what you have seen so far is only an introduction to these things. In due time they will be explained further."

The story resumes at chapter six.

The Narrow Road

Enter through the narrow gate. For wide is the gate and broad is the road that leads to destruction, and many enter through it. But small is the gate and narrow the road that leads to life, and only a few find it.

—JESUS, MATTHEW 7:13–14

Two Destinies

"There was a rich man who was dressed in purple and fine linen and lived in luxury every day. At his gate was laid a beggar named Lazarus, covered with sores and longing to eat what fell from the rich man's table. Even the dogs came and licked his sores.

"The time came when the beggar died and the angels carried him to Abraham's side. The rich man also died and was buried. In hell, where he was in torment, he looked up and saw Abraham far away, with Lazarus by his side. So he called to him, 'Father Abraham, have pity on me and send Lazarus to dip the tip of his finger in water and cool my tongue, because I am in agony in this fire.'

"But Abraham replied, 'Son, remember that in your lifetime you received your good things, while Lazarus received bad things, but now he is comforted here and you are in agony. And besides all this, between us and you a great chasm has been fixed, so that those who want to go from here to you cannot, nor can anyone cross over from there to us.'

"He answered, 'Then I beg you, father, send Lazarus to my father's house, for I have five brothers. Let him warn them, so that they will not also come to this place of torment.'

"Abraham replied, 'They have Moses and the Prophets; let them listen to them.'

"'No, father Abraham,' he said, 'but if someone from the dead goes to them, they will repent.'

"He said to him, 'If they do not listen to Moses and the Prophets, they will not be convinced even if someone rises from the dead.'"

—JESUS, LUKE 16:19–31

Do Not Ignore It

How shall we escape if we ignore such a great salvation? This salvation, which was first announced by the Lord, was confirmed to us by those who heard him. God also testified to it by signs, wonders and various miracles, and gifts of the Holy Spirit distributed according to his will.

—HEBREWS 2:3–4

The Holy City

I did not see a temple in the city, because the Lord God Almighty and the Lamb are its temple. The city does not need the sun or the moon to shine on it, for the glory of God gives it light, and the Lamb is its lamp. The nations will walk by its light, and the kings of the earth will bring their splendor into it. On no day will its gates ever be shut, for there will be no night there. The glory and honor of the nations will be brought into it. Nothing impure will ever enter it, nor will anyone who does what is shameful or deceitful, but only those whose names are written in the Lamb's book of life.

—JOHN, REVELATION 21:22–27

Reigning With God

Then the angel showed me the river of the water of life, as clear as crystal, flowing from the throne of God and of the Lamb down the middle of the great street of the city. On each side of the river stood the tree of life, bearing twelve crops of fruit, yielding its fruit every month. And the leaves of the tree are for the healing of the nations. No longer will there be any curse. The throne of God and of the Lamb will be in the city, and his servants will serve him. They will see his face, and his name will be on their foreheads. There will be no more night. They will not need the light of a lamp or the light of the sun, for the Lord God will give them light. And they will reign for ever and ever.

—JOHN, REVELATION 22:1–5

Finally

This story has resurrected the timeless question: "What happens to us when we die?" Society taboos make us reluctant to ask it, but it is a question that will not go away.

We have read about remarkable scenes of heaven and hell that seem strange to our earth-bound minds. As strange as they may seem, the recurring theme of how we can secure peace with God and eternal life with Him in heaven is solidly consistent with the timeless and oft told gospel message.

Look again at some of these extracts from the story:

The old man: *"Look what redeeming grace has done."*

The angels reprimand of Marietta: *"I have to warn you about your former unbelief and your lack of faith and dedication. For there is no other way, apart from Christ, the Redeemer, to find an inheritance in this place."*

Marietta's cry in hell: *"Oh! If I could only have one hour back on earth—for a time, just a brief time— to prepare my soul and make me fit for heaven."*

Jesus' words: *"I came so that salvation may be given to the world, and that everyone... might obtain forgiveness and eternal life through faith and repentance."*

Finally, from Justice: *"...the sinner will be restored through repentance towards God and faith in the Lord Jesus."*

The story has done far more than awaken us to the world beyond—it has given the priceless knowledge and opportunity to make peace with God, to have a life with Him on earth, and an eternal life in heaven.

Today can be the greatest day of your life, as you *"enter through the narrow gate"* to meet God and begin eternity with Him.

The way is simple, as described above. Repent of your past wrongdoings and, by faith, accept the forgiveness Jesus gained for you. You can do this by this simple prayer:

Lord God, I acknowledge that I have sinned against you. I am sorry for this and I now choose to change my ways—please help me to do so. I gratefully accept Your forgiveness and Spirit in my life. I thank You that I am now Your child. I will serve You for the rest of my life and for eternity.

Chapter 3
Welcome in Heaven

1. The winepress usually refers to the judgment of God.

Chapter 4
First Lessons and Warnings

1. See Revelation 7:9–17.

Chapter 9
The Intellectual, the False Teacher, and the Heartless Worshipers

1. See Matthew 23:27.
2. See Romans 3:4.

Chapter 11
The Music of Heaven and the Separation

1. This incident is included in the three sections in Appendix B.
2. See Revelation 21, particularly verse 27.
3. See Luke 16:26.
4. See 1 John 3:9–10.

5. A reference to Zechariah 13. This passage foretells the coming of Christ the Shepherd who would come and die, shedding His blood to bring cleansing from sin.

6. See Revelation 7:9–15.

Chapter 12

Infant Instruction—the Lost Man

1. Remember that this was written well before the advent of movies or television. Marietta takes the next paragraph to explain a process that was probably analogous to what today we see on a screen, or perhaps via the media of virtual reality.

Chapter 14

The Justice-Mercy Conflict

1. See Hebrews 1:8; Daniel 4:3, 34; 7:27; Psalm 119:89.

2. See Hebrews 13:12. Jesus suffering "outside the city gate" signified the removal of sin from the city.

3. The Son of David was one of the Old Testament titles of the coming Messiah—meaning a descendant of David. See Isaiah 9:6–7; Malachi 4:2; Matthew 1:1; Revelation 22:16.

Chapter 15

The Judas Betrayal

1. See John 16:16.

2. See John 16:6–7.

3. See John 14:18.

4. See John 14:1–3.

5. See John 14:19.

6. See John 16:20.

7. See John 16:22.

8. See John 16:25.

9. See Matthew 23:37–24:2. Jerusalem and the temple were destroyed about forty years later in A.D. 70, as Jesus had

predicted, by the Romans.

    10. See Matthew 23:16.

    11. See Matthew 23:13.

    12. See Matthew 26:38, 41.

    13. See Luke 22:44.

    14. See Luke 4:18–19.

Chapter 17

Apollyon

    1. *Apollyon* is one of the several names of Satan. It appears in Revelation 9:11, and means *destroyer*.

Chapter 20

The Thirty Pieces of Silver

1. See Romans 8:7.

Chapter 22

Death Defeated

1. See John 19:11.

Chapter 23

He Is Risen!

1. See John 15:20; 16:33.

2. See Luke 24:49 and Acts 2:1–4.

3. See Revelation 4:8.

4. See Revelation 22:13

Chapter 24

The Lost Man Rescued

    1. See Leviticus 25:8–55 and Luke 4:19. In ancient Israel in the year of Jubilee (every fiftieth year) slaves were freed,

debts were cancelled, and ancestral property was returned to the original owner. Here the liberation is from sin and all its consequences.

2. See John 5:24.

3. See Ephesians 6:11–18.

4. See Luke 10:2.

5. See Matthew 10:8.

6. See Hebrews 13:15.

7. See Psalm 139:23–24.